Soul Scream

The End Was Just The Beginning

My Life. My Story. God's Plan.

By
S. Nikki Creque

Edited by
Thomas Gette

Thanks and Glory to Yahweh, first and foremost for giving me strength and showing me my purpose.

Thank you Mom and Dad for loving and supporting me through everything no matter what.

This book is dedicated to Chelsea, Alexander and Nils

It's no mistake the first letters of your name in the order of your birth spell the word 'CAN'.
With Yahweh first
You CAN be anything.
You CAN do anything.
And I will always love you no matter what simply because, I CAN.

Love Mom

CONTENTS

Introduction 1

Chapter 1 5
It Had To End To Begin

Chapter 2 11
No Regrets

Chapter 3 30
Looking Ahead

Chapter 4 40
Lesson 1: Learning To Learn

Chapter 5 50
Lesson 2: Giving It All To Him

Chapter 6 75
Lesson 3: A Blessing May Come In Not Getting What You Desire

Chapter 7 83
Lesson 4: Determining Who You're Destined To Be and Pursuing It

Chapter 8 96
Lesson 5: Surround Yourself With The Right People Of Accountability

Chapter 9 114
You'll Feel Better After You Scream

Note From The Author 128

INTRODUCTION

> For I know the plans I have for you, says the LORD, plans for welfare and not for evil, to give you a future and a hope. (Jeremiah 29:11-14)

#

Of all the times I feel a surge to write, it has to be while I'm walking through the Miami-Dade Airport, having just left my best friend after spending five days in beautiful Charlotte Amalie, St. Thomas (courtesy of her for my birthday). But somehow all I can hear as I traipse towards my terminal is my brother's voice in my head telling me over and over again that I must write my story, I must finish it, and I must accomplish the things that I have laid out to accomplish.

There are so many things that I have wanted to do (we all seem to have an endless list of the many great accomplishments that we want to achieve). Very few of these things have stayed fixated in my mind long enough to get completed. The rest of them –they've died– slowly, but surely. However, this one thing that I've shared with my brother, he has backed me on one hundred percent, and he has kept its fire burning, even when I've let it dwindle out to a flicker. That is, this story.

Soul SCREAM: The End Was Just The Beginning
Introduction

As I sit here waiting for my flight so that I can head home to my children, I write this book. I don't know why I write it. I don't know. Maybe it's because I want to find the income to move my family away from the turmoil that they experience where we live now. Or could it be that I am truly writing it to share my story with others who have felt this much pain and sorrow so that they can find a means to peace like I have? I guess I won't know until I'm done.

Yet, one thing I do know for sure, the words are coming and they won't stop, and I only have one choice but to write them down.

I find myself a corner in between terminals ten and eight trying to find some quiet so that I can speak the words that will fill this book. I know that some will stare at me oddly as I sit here on my phone talking to myself, them not knowing why I'm saying what I'm saying or whether I am actually talking to someone, but the small glimpse that they catch is in fact a door into a whole other world, my world.

That's okay, because the words that I will speak, that will be written, shall be read by many, that I know for sure. It doesn't scare me what they will think of me at the end of this, it doesn't scare me how people will view me.

I suppose I've reached a point where I have no more fear, and I simply have love for myself and others. It's that point where you

Soul SCREAM: The End Was Just The Beginning
Introduction

stop wherever you are, look up to the heavens, lift your hands and just scream.

Scream for all the pain you've ever felt. Scream for all the people who are afraid of doing it themselves. And scream because the pain and hurt you feel is so great that you no longer know who you are, what you are doing, and where you are going.

After the screaming has commenced, you desire no more to cry or fight or scream. I have reached this point, and it's literally been drawn out of me by the people who felt compelled to judge and condemn me. Moreover, it has become especially clear from seeing through unshielded eyes the consequences of the decisions that I have made.

My scream, I believe, was heard by the angels, Christ, and God. When I had finished and my strength was gone, He sent the angels down to protect to me, to heal me, and awaken my soul to all that He has wanted of me and has waited for me to become. I was finally ready for Him to rebuild me into what and who He wanted me to be.

What I desired no longer mattered. I gave it all to him and trusted that he would make me greater than I could ever imagine. I didn't need to know how it would be accomplished; all I knew was that it had begun.

Soul SCREAM: The End Was Just The Beginning
Introduction

I spoke to my ex-husband a couple of days ago, and he said that he cannot understand why I ask what I ask and why I do what I do. The truth of the matter is that he does not understand because he chooses not to, and that is his choice. Even if he did make the choice to try and understand me, maybe he wouldn't.

There are certain trials and tribulations of ours that God does not want others to understand, and they are what He uses to teach us and help us grow. My ex-husband would no more understand mine as I would the ones given to him.

So, as I share with you my lessons, my life, my tears, my heartbreak, my love, and my metamorphosis, I hope that you will come to understand your own life and find your own need for love and learn your own lessons from your trials and tribulations.

If one person can get from my book a deeper understanding of who they're meant to be in God's name and it allows them to open themselves up to Him in various new ways, then I will have accomplished exactly what I was meant to do.

CHAPTER {1}

It Had To End To Begin

\#

It was a cold November morning. My husband, who had been with me for fifteen years, five of which we were married, woke up, knocked on my door, and told me that he was moving out. He had already reserved a moving truck. He proceeded to ask me what items he could take.

I knew this was coming, I just didn't know when. I thought he would give me a little bit more time to prepare. I mean, even though he had filed for divorce three months ago, we had been up and down and fought and been through nonsense.

I just wasn't ready to let him go, which is so ironic considering the fact that I hadn't been home much. I had been everywhere but home. I had been back and forth to my mother's house twenty minutes away, I had been back and forth to her business, and I spent time with my brother's girlfriend (by then my brother had been deceased a year or two).

I was running errands for my sister, I was being a support for my brother, and I was taking care of my grandmother and my father. The only thing I that wasn't doing was taking care of myself and my husband. I wasn't taking care of my home.

Soul SCREAM: The End Was Just The Beginning
Chapter 1

I couldn't believe that he was going to leave me. That he was going to walk out that door, take his stuff, and leave me. "You don't leave me, I leave you," were the words that came out of my mouth eventually. After being hurt, after trying to explain myself, after trying to apologize for not being there for him, for not being everything that he needed (even though I tried to be), I just didn't know what the rest of it was.

It was like the list that I had been given somewhere in my lifeline didn't quite match with the list that he had. I had done my best, but my best in his book was not good enough.

I didn't know what else to do but to turn and let him go. We had built this beautiful home, had three beautiful children, and had fought for fifteen years to keep what we had. The material items didn't mean anything anymore. There was a point when I thought that if we bought the first house I would be happy, but I wasn't. I thought that if we built a bigger house I'd be happy, but I wasn't. I thought that if he got a better job and made more money that I would be happy, but I wasn't.

I look at all the things that he's jumped through to make me happy. He became somebody that I'm not sure he really was in the beginning. Honestly, I didn't know because I wasn't sure who I was. All I knew was change had come and it was scaring the hell out of me.

Soul SCREAM: The End Was Just The Beginning
Chapter 1

I could see the look on my children's faces that he paid no mind to. I could see the quiver in my son's hands as his father told him to go get his stuff.

As I stood in my garage door, I watched the truck pull away with my husband and my two sons. My daughter was mine from a previous relationship, and although he claimed her as his own, I just couldn't let her go that day. I felt like if I let her go I was letting him take everything.

I was wrong. If she wanted to leave I should have let her. That is her dad. So, I let them go and I stood there with her. She walked back into the house and cried silently in her room. I, on the other hand, didn't make it that far.

I walked into the house, got to the front door, and stared at it realizing that he would not be walking through that door at six o'clock after work anymore, that the kids would not come running down the steps to greet him as they always did, and that I would not hear somebody walk into the kitchen and say as he always would, "That smells absolutely horrible, I don't think you should feed that to anybody else but me."

I fell to my knees with tears in my eyes and for the first time in almost ten years I prayed. I prayed like I had never prayed before. I prayed about things I had done. I prayed about things I hadn't done. I prayed about things that I wanted to have done. I just prayed.

After I had finished praying, I had this sick feeling in the bottomless pit of my stomach. I picked myself up off the floor, went upstairs, and lay down in the bed that I had shared with him for so many years. I thought that when we bought a king-sized bed it would be the best thing ever to have a bed that the whole family could fit into.

The only problem was, once the children became a certain age they left our bed and it left a gap, a huge gap between me and him. I had at times tried to roll over into that gap to be closer to him, but for some reason I always rolled back to my side. We would meet in the middle sometimes, but we never stayed there, we always went back to our respective sides.

Anybody who would ask me now about getting a king-sized bed, I would tell them that it could potentially damage their marriage. I believe that you need a queen- sized bed to be able to be close, to feel the heat from the body next to you of the person whom you adore, whom you love. That heat is a constant reminder. It keeps alive the flame within your body and within your heart for that person, letting you know that they are there.

Even in the months before when he had moved into the guest room, I would knock on the door and ask to sleep with him because I simply could not get used to sleeping alone. Even years into the future after the divorce, I would keep clean laundry on the side of my bed to give me the impression of a body being there.

Soul SCREAM: The End Was Just The Beginning
Chapter 1

The only difference was that the bed remained very cold, so, while it took up space, it didn't give me that warmth.

As I lay in the bed that night knowing that he was not under this roof with his family and that my sons were sleeping in a shell of a house that they were moving into, I cried. I had been taught to never show weakness and to never show fear, but in this given moment I didn't know what else to do.

I think I got out of bed between nine that night and five the next morning roughly five times, and I prayed each time I rolled over that he would be there looking at me the way he used to, telling me that he was going to try, try to see the splinter of a marriage that we had left, but every time I rolled over he wasn't there, he ceased to exist at my bedside.

Contrary to before, I now know that perfection is not possible. I know that it takes a lot more than a vow and a ring and a smile to keep a marriage going. I know now that God did not want this for me. How do I know this? I know this because God would never have sent another man into my life for me to have an affair with while I was the wife of another man. Would he?? I was so confused.

My soul was broken, my heart was torn, but it was in those few seconds and moments that I realized I didn't know who I had become after all those years. Had I or did I really love this man or was this just my ego hurt over losing him?

Soul SCREAM: The End Was Just The Beginning
Chapter 1

My life was about to change and I was about to hit rock bottom and be rebuilt by God's hands Himself.

I had no idea what was coming or how it was going to come, but whatever it was, it had just begun.

CHAPTER {2}

No Regrets

#

Okay, all drama aside, you read right, your eyes didn't deceive you. I had a big fat juicy affair, at least by everyone else's standard. Now before you go judging me and throwing stones, for those of you with your hands up ready to aim, I ask you to keep an open mind and hear me out. I know there is no acceptable justification, per say for cheating so I won't waste my time giving you one.

I'll just say I did it because at the time I wanted to. Point blank, plain and simple. So why would this housewife with a so called 'perfect life' to others, a good husband, who was a great provider and considered a good father, decide to go this route? Answer, I wasn't happy. Honestly, I think miserable is a more appropriate description.

Oh, I'm sorry, were you expecting some deep mind altering drawn out response? Well I'm sorry, I don't have one and quite honestly, I stopped handing those out a while ago along with apologies for this whole situation and how my divorce affected my family and those around me. No matter how much remorse I showed some people still saw me as this horrible person who wasn't supposed to ever make a mistake in her life.

Soul SCREAM: The End Was Just The Beginning
Chapter 2

If I knew people had me on such a high pedestal, I would have asked to have been removed from it previously. Nobody's perfect, we're all human, so I personally don't believe in pedestals but to each his own. I didn't plan any of what happened, it just did and here's how.

When I was married I had the 2 car garage house, financial stability and pretty much whatever I wanted, but I still felt like I was empty and missing something in my life. I went above and beyond to be a good wife, mother, daughter and friend to everyone, but I always felt no matter what I did that it just wasn't appreciated and valued by others as much as I'd have liked, including my own husband.

A significant part of my life basically revolved around modifying my behavior, my appearance and my actions to please others. This behavior was a direct result of some things that took place in my childhood but we're not going to dive into that. I don't have enough time to write about it and you don't have enough time to read it. That's another book in itself, if not a TV mini-series. So let's move on.

When it came to my marriage and my household I ran everything. I definitely wore the pants in the marriage, but I think he gave them to me because back then if he didn't I'd have a tantrum out of this world until he did. Some men would stand their ground, but he backed down to keep the peace not knowing that each time he backed down, I lost a little more respect for him. Crazy but true.

Soul SCREAM: The End Was Just The Beginning
Chapter 2

If he spoke up and tried to lead in our house, as he should of, it was cool as long as I agreed but if I didn't I went off to keep my control and he backed down. When he backed down I saw him as weak for not standing his ground with me. Sounds crazy but some women will understand where I'm coming from. You know how it is, when your man is quiet and civil so when we argue with him we beat him down with our words.

And then one day he speaks up, stands his ground, taking no more of our mouth and as a result we find him even more attractive than we did when we first met. Again, crazy but true. I was a grown spoiled and controlling wife- brat and if my husband stepped to me I attacked him with little to no remorse. In my defense, I grew up having seen this so I didn't see anything wrong with at that time in my life. This was our marriage for years until one day it started to change because I started to change.

Now before you go skimming ahead seeking the name of the man who sparked this change and who woke me up from my boring monotonous life, I'll let you know I'm not using his real name. Considering everyone knows everyone in my home state, I'm going to call him Cameron for the sake of privacy, Cam for short.

Only a few know who he is and I'd like to keep it that way. Sorry ladies, I know you'll be dying to know by the end of this chapter and I would tell you except I failed sharing in Pre-K. So sorry ladies;)

Chapter 2

Let's shoot back to the past first. Cam and I went to high school together but became really good friends during the last two years. After high school, we lost touch of course but one day during Christmas break 2010, I ran into him around our hometown.

I'm going to be honest and disclose that even when I was in high school I had a huge crush on Cam. He was good looking in high school and kind of corny but now as a grown man "he was all that and a bag of chips". Forgive me, I know I just told my age with that comment, but it is what it is and well, it's the truth.

He was even more handsome now with a tall slim muscular build. His skin tone to me was between a Morris Chestnut and a Taye Diggs. Now if you don't know who they are please find the receipt for this book and return it NOW. You are not allowed to read any further if you don't know who those beautiful specimens of the black male species are. All others, you may proceed.

As he walked over to me I tried not to let my face reflect what my brain was thinking and my body was trying not to do. I stood there as my eyes drank in his Greek God like physique, milk chocolate skin and suddenly locked eyes with his light brown eyes. Let's just say that was all she wrote.

I was instantly thrown back to high school memories and I started to remember how he would pick and tease with me and others at the lunch table during my freshmen and sophomore years. I always felt like the awkward one out in my high school clique and felt as though he targeted me the most. It could have been wishful thinking but this is my story, my book and my memory so I'm keeping my memory just the way it is.

Cameron would come over to our table and joke and tease me and whoever else was sitting there but unlike them while they complained I was subconsciously begging for more of his attention, good or bad. It didn't matter to me as long as I was getting it. To this day, I don't think I've ever shared my feelings with him and I'd never have dared tell him any of this during high school. During our senior year I played the role of the 'cool female' friend.

That was always my M.O. in high school. I didn't care too much to be friends with too many girls because they were always so catty and it gave me joy to see their faces scowled up when I walked by in the protection of the cute guys they wished would just say hello to them once.

Cam had a girlfriend junior and senior year and while my teen-self used to look for reasons why he shouldn't be with her, my adult self must admit that she was genuinely a nice and down to earth person. She never saw me as a threat because I was after all the 'cool female' friend. Right?

Senior year we had a senior dance and I for the life of me couldn't get a date. Let me rephrase that, I couldn't get a date I wanted. I can't remember exactly if I asked Cameron to go with me or if he suggested in pity because I had no date. I'm going to guess that I asked him because I was straightforward like that even back then.

Well we went to the dance and let me tell you, he looked amazing in the cream suit jacket and black pants he wore to coordinate with my cream and gold dress. We had a so much fun with friends and it was a great night. After he dropped me off I ran in the house and into my room as quick I could. My room was at the front of the house so any car driving by could see right in my window if the shutters were completely open.

After making sure the shutters were wide open and I proceeded to get undressed knowing that when he backed down the driveway and drove past the front of the house, he would have no choice but to catch a glimpse of my beautiful virgin body. Man I was such a typical teenage girl.

His car did pause at the end of the drive way for a few minutes before he pulled off but to this day I have no idea if he saw me or not parading around in my bra and panties. And now 16 years later, here he was standing right in front of me a whole grown milk chocolate man. OMG! As I approached him I had my signature stupid grin on my face.

Anyone who knows me knows the one I'm talking about. I silently prayed in my head, "God please don't let me turn into that corny girl from high school!" Thank goodness I had some self-control and didn't.

We had a great conversation about where we were in life and exchanged numbers promising to keep in touch. I remember

Soul SCREAM: The End Was Just The Beginning
Chapter 2

looking at that number days later and didn't think I would ever hear from or see him again. Boy was I wrong.

He had moved out of state some time ago and had only been in town visiting family for the holidays. I actually didn't hear from him for close to 3 weeks after and then one day I was floored to see a text from him on my phone. I mean who bumps into old friends and actually keeps in touch when they say they're going to?

We started texting and speaking regularly from that day on. He worked an overnight shift so most nights I spoke to him while he was working so I would get out of bed and go downstairs so I wouldn't keep my husband up while I was on the phone.

It was crazy how we hadn't seen each other in years, but we spoke as if it had just been days or weeks running down to each other how our lives had progressed since high school. We talked about everything you could imagine and it was awesome.

For some reason I opened up to Cam like he was my best girlfriend or something. It was kind of weird but also very cool. My husband and I had built a house about 40 minutes outside of town at this time so while the kids were at school I was either home bored or working a few hours helping my mom at her daycare center.

I was starving for adult conversation during the week since my husband and all my friends worked full-time. I started to look forward to Cameron's call and our conversations each night.

Soul SCREAM: The End Was Just The Beginning
Chapter 2

After about a month of us communicating it didn't take a genius to see the connection we had and the attraction that had developed between us. I tried to ignore it at first but at this time in my marriage my husband and I weren't doing so well.

We had gone close to six months without intimacy and I honestly thought he may be cheating. It was so bad I literally resorted to asking him to schedule nights for us to have sex. I had seen on Oprah one day a wife and husband who had done the same and it revitalized their marriage. Of course he objected stating that it wouldn't feel natural to do so.

All I remember thinking to myself was if he also felt that it was natural to go 6 months without sex. Forget natural, I was starving for attention, sex and intimacy.

What I didn't realize at the time though was that my texting and phone calls with Cameron were filling my need for attention and creating in me a desire for intimacy from him not my husband. I believe that's why I reached out to my husband like I did because I could feel my heart's direction starting to change and I was trying to stop it.

Not only were Cam and I growing emotionally close through our time conversing, we both were at a point in our lives where we weren't happy with our relationships and we wanted to make changes. The same effect he had over me in high school he still was having over me years later while we spoke over the phone and it felt good.

Soul SCREAM: The End Was Just The Beginning
Chapter 2

We shared with each other our goals, ambitions and dreams. It was amazing how much we had in common. I think we were actually finding out more about each other now than we did when we were in high school and it was really cool. On the phone with him each night I felt so alive as if I'd been sleepwalking through life before he and I reconnected. This was how my husband used to make me feel but hadn't in such a long time. Cam was meeting my needs and doing it without even knowing that he was.

Cameron wanted to talk to me. Cameron wanted to text with me. Cameron wanted me and like an insect flying straight into the light, I loved it and didn't want it to stop.

He became my best friend all over again and I shared with him things about myself I hadn't even told my girlfriends or husband. I was getting to know this grownup version of him and to me he was just amazing. He had a drive to achieve his goals like no other person I knew. I envied him because while he was trying to reach his goals I was sitting at home with my goals on the back burner and my kids and husband's goals on the front burner. I felt stuck with no purpose and of no importance to the people around me.

Seeing Cameron in this new light at this point in my life made his worth and potential shine even brighter to me and I was absolutely starting to fall for this guy all over again.

He was constantly motivating me to set goals and start working towards them to find my purpose but most importantly he believed I was meant to achieve more and wanted me to open my mind to new ideas and concepts to do so. I loved his fresh approach to life and I was sold on the fact that not only did I love this man that I could accomplish great things with him.

I made plans to fly out and visit him and I figured I'd go visit other family in the state while I was there as well. Why I was so nervous I don't know. I guess I thought that once he saw me in person he would see that awkward girl from high school, his attraction would disappear and I would spend the remainder of my trip touring museums and landmarks by myself.

I mean look at me, I had three kids and while I would never classify myself as fat I definitely was bigger than I used to be. Looking at how attractive Cam was I was sure that he was into the supermodel, video vixen type chicks. Whatever attraction I felt we had over the phone I was starting to doubt exist.

I flew out to see him and shortly after I got checked into my hotel he called to let me know he was coming up to the room. I became nervous beyond belief and I must have checked my hair, face and makeup like 5 times over the next 10 minutes. My heart damn near skipped a beat when I heard the knock at the hotel room door. On the way walking to open the room door I tried to calm the hyper teenage girl jumping around within me.

As soon as our eyes met instantly I felt calm, warm and safe standing there in front of him and when he hugged me I just melted in his arms like milk chocolate.

Soul SCREAM: The End Was Just The Beginning
Chapter 2

It was absolutely crazy because I thought I was going to be nervous or on the defensive but I did just the opposite, with him I just dropped my guard and relinquished control over to him. You would think he'd put a spell on me or something because I never dropped my guard like that for anyone, not even my husband.

For the first time in a long time, I felt completely safe with Cameron to fall back, act like a lady and let him be the man and lead. I really don't know how else to explain it. I wanted him to take the lead and I wanted to follow. I felt so safe and protected with him and it felt good.

His strength, intelligence and the way he carried himself was awe-inspiring to me. I felt privileged to be the woman at his side. I was ready to walk next to him, beside him, behind him, I didn't care where as long as I was with him and he was with me. I could care less about anyone or anything else at that moment.

Now I know what some of you may be thinking and you're wrong. The attraction between wasn't just lust, it was real and was rooted by our friendship. We genuinely cared about and loved each other. The physical attraction though between us was quite unbelievable, unlike any attraction I've ever experienced before towards any other man.

It made me feel like we were truly meant for each other, like soulmates. When our eyes locked it was like I could read his thoughts which weren't always sexual, but when they were it was, as I like to say, game on.

Chapter 2

Time stopped for us when we were together and nothing else mattered at that moment but us. There were no distractions that could break us gazing into each other's eyes. I can't tell you how many pieces of clothing I've had destroyed at the start of and during our lovemaking sessions. If my clothing was a hindrance to him in any way, he'd just rip it off like a tiger tearing through the skin of his prey to get to the flesh beneath.

The first time this happened our eyes were so intensely locked that I didn't even notice or feel him doing it. Afterwards, I was shocked that I had become so entranced and hadn't even tried to prevent him from destroying my poor dress. The power Cam had over me felt good, felt right.

When he touched my body it did things I didn't tell it to do. Things I didn't want it to do, at least not yet. It was as if my body had a mind of its own and he was its master and my body his willing submissive. He stared straight into my soul with his brown eyes. No words were needed sometimes; just a glance and my body knew what he wanted from it and free will went out the window. Even as

I type this I shake my head because I still can't understand how anyone can affect another person like he did me.

Here I was this strong, independent-thinking, intelligent woman who was a leader to those around me but with him one look made me want to fall into his arms.

Soul SCREAM: The End Was Just The Beginning
Chapter 2

Sometimes my mind would be telling me to speak, but my lips only did and said what he wanted. And when we weren't making love in the bedroom, the car or some other spontaneous place, which I absolutely loved, we were the best of friends just like in high school. I respected him, he respected me and we had so fun together.

It felt great to be appreciated and see my value reflected back at me through his eyes, actions and affection towards me. I didn't have to fight for his attention nor try and act in a way I thought he wanted to get it. Begging for time and affection from my husband had become so routine but with Cam it was given so freely without any rules, restrictions or requirements.

When I was in town I was his priority and he never missed an opportunity to show me this. For so long I had been starved of the things that I was receiving from Cam that at first I didn't quite know how to give them back but he was patient with me and little by little I was learning to reciprocate them back. As I progressed in this area I started to feel the protective ice I had built around myself and my heart start to melt.

He was helping me discover a whole new side of myself I had never known, a side that I had lost and forgotten about over the years. It felt amazing uncovering this lost part of me again and even though it was wrong, I loved every minute of it, every minute of being with him.

I kept telling myself that God must have seen how unhappy I was and had sent this man back in my life to show me the kind of relationship I was deserving of. Or that Cameron was my soul mate and he being brought back into my life again was proof of that.

The way I felt about Cam was different from anything I had ever felt, even with my husband. Cam made me feel safe protected like he would never let anyone or anything harm me. I wanted to feel protected with my husband but the truth was that my husband had failed me in that area of our relationship many times over the years.

Instead of having my back or validating the feelings I was experiencing due to various situations or people, he told me to let them go and move on or that I was over-reacting. When my husband proposed to me for years I kept pushing the date back because deep inside something just didn't feel right. I didn't know why but I felt I wasn't ready yet and I just needed more time.

When Cam came back in my life I realized then that I should never have gotten married with how I felt at the time. I did what others said was right because we had children together, but it didn't feel a hundred percent right. This felt right, plain and simple. Cameron felt right.

Being with Cam didn't require anything extra work from me for him or his family, it just felt naturally like a good fit and we flowed like yin and yang. His mother already knew me from high school and I loved her and she loved me.

Soul SCREAM: The End Was Just The Beginning
Chapter 2

So where's Cam now? Honestly, I don't know. I made plans to divorce my husband, pack my kids up, move and start a whole new life with Cam. I didn't care about what others thought or said, I felt like I deserved this fresh start and had earned this opportunity for true happiness with someone I had always wanted to be with even before I met my husband.

I mean let's keep it real, had my husband not given me an ultimatum to set a wedding date because I was taking so long doing so, I'm not certain we would have ended up married in the first place. I wasn't ready but I was terrified at the thought of raising my kids by myself and becoming statistically know as a 'baby mama'. To this day I absolutely dislike that title.

I don't care what people say and how many kids you have with someone, if you're not moved to marry them or something doesn't feel right, don't do it. You can be a good parent without being married.

As parents we are living examples to our children and if they see us in an unhappy relationship day in and day out then they'll be inclined to do the same when they get older. My kids have told me repeatedly since I've been divorced, how much happier and positive I am and I have to agree, I am happier. They even told me because of this new happiness I've been a better parent.

My marriage wasn't horrible, we had a lot of great times but no matter how hard I tried to make it work it just wasn't a good fit for me. My divorce was so treacherous that the negativity from it started to spill out onto the people around me whom I cared about.

My friends and family started being questioned about whether they had knowledge of my affair. I had been discreet with everyone but once my husband found out discreetness went out the window and my phone was ringing off the hook with people wanting to know what had happened.

No one had known and as it started to come out amongst family and friends I got a first-hand taste of how quick people are to judge and condemn others with no questions asked. When I disclosed to my family and my husband's family that I was taking my kids and moving out of state, all hell broke loose, literally. In the span of three short months, my life became a nightmare filled with court dates, lawyer's fees, nasty arguments and threats to target and harm Cam anyway they could if I moved.

When things progressed to this point, I made the decision to cut Cam and anyone associated with him completely off. I even cancelled all my social media pages for about a year. Honestly, it was the only way I could protect my kids, myself and Cameron from my great big mess.

I knew I couldn't fake cutting him off because I was under so much scrutiny that I couldn't go on a road trip much less take a flight without fifty questions about where I was going and why. I never told him or gave warning, I just did it. I wasn't about to have him be judged and crucified for my decisions and actions when he wasn't the married one, I was.

Soul SCREAM: The End Was Just The Beginning
Chapter 2

To add insult to injury, I allowed people, who claimed to have my best interests in mind, get in my head and start planting seeds of negativity concerning my relationship and friendship with Cam. They told me that he was using me and that men as attractive as him don't settle down with nice ordinary girls like me.

This coupled with my low self-esteem at the time literally turned me into this mentally weak woman who now doubted everything I felt for Cameron and whether he had actually cared at all for me. I spent many sleepless nights awake replaying our conversations and all the time we spent together, looking for anything to support what they were saying.

Over analyzing people and situations is what Virgos do, usually to an extreme which is exactly what I did. Before I knew it I found myself taking antidepressants to try and get my mind off of it and just stop thinking at all.

Even though I was still married and was living under the same roof as my husband, for me the emotional, physical and mental connection between my husband and I had been severed for a while. I had done such a good job of faking my happiness over the past year and trying to please everyone and no one knew or could tell except our kids.

With Cam I didn't have to fake my happiness, not even back in high school, it was real. Now my actions were out and everyone was looking for someone to blame. They zeroed right in on Cameron and the crazy part is I never told him, thinking I was protecting him and I don't believe he had any idea that he was being made the villain in all of this.

It hurt, but letting him go and any thought of a future with him was what I had to do. I was so emotionally and mentally unbalanced, I had to do it and I have no regrets. Anyone who is lucky enough to get the title friend from me knows that my true friends are my family for life and I'm always there for them no matter what or when they call on me. One thing I do know for sure is that you can't keep two people who are meant to be together apart.

It doesn't matter how long it takes or what you do or say. If you're meant to be with someone you will always find each other no matter how long or how far away you are from each other. Eventually you will be with them or spend the rest of the life thinking about them time to time wondering how they're doing. I truly believe that two people can be fated to be together and no one can make me think any differently about this.

So where is Cam? Cameron is where Cameron is and I am where I am. When the time comes if we're meant to be, we'll find each other and I believe it will be like no time has passed and we will still feel as strongly about each other as we did before. Do I have any regrets? I used to, but I don't anymore. If I had chosen a different path you wouldn't be reading this book, so you're welcome. I do sometimes wish

Soul SCREAM: The End Was Just The Beginning
Chapter 2

I had fought harder for my happiness and new life with him, but I also believe everything happens for a reason and the timing wasn't right. My sacrifice wasn't in vain though and neither was his. I know he's out there somewhere and I'm sure he's okay but trust, if he wasn't I'd know.

Any man or woman, who's ever used the word 'love' and meant it, knows exactly what I'm saying. Don't you? That's how the law of attraction works. Nothing that is truly meant to be together can be kept apart. Only time will truly tell in which way this applies or doesn't to us. And, believe me that will be whole 'nother' book.

Until then the clock keeps ticking and I have work to do. Tick tock.....

CHAPTER {3}

LOOKING AHEAD

#

It has been five years since my marriage ended. When I look back, I am shocked at who and where I was in my life then. My life is so different and absolutely amazing today. Unfortunately, like many divorcees, I was forced to leave my home and move. In an attempt to foster a better parenting relationship, I moved into a townhouse less than two miles from my estranged husband.

He had chosen to move into a townhouse back in my home state where we met. It was only twenty-five minutes from where we were living the past seven years, but it still meant that the kids had to leave their friends, school and home, which was very difficult for them. I tried to convince my husband to sign off on papers letting me stay in the house until our twin sons turned eighteen, but he was against it and refused.

I understood his reasoning, which was that he wanted to let the house go so that he could start his new life.

I really wanted what was best for the kids, though, having felt guilty that it was my actions and decisions that had caused an end to come to what they considered their perfect childhood. Even though I understood his choice, I still felt that he made the decision based on trying to punish me for hurting him with my infidelity. It was, even more, painful watching our children hurting as a result of getting caught in the middle of everything going on around them and not having any voice in it at all.

My new home and neighborhood turned out to be a blessing in disguise. It has taken three years for the kids to finally stop asking to move back 'home'. Our twin sons are in the eighth grade and will be entering high school next fall, and our amazing daughter will be starting college. When we first moved I was working with my mother at her business. The stress of the divorce and working with my mother wasn't easy.

I started being late to work frequently because, honestly, I just couldn't find the physical nor mental strength to get out of bed some mornings. This is where my kids stepped in and became the source of my strength and motivation. No matter what I was going through I had decided that I had to be a rock for them, you know, that one person whom no matter what they could depend upon and trust to be there for them.

I had been, for the most part, their primary caretaker for their entire lives, and after having lost their father living in the home, I knew they couldn't handle it if I and our routine changed too much too quickly. So each morning I would get up with a smile, make breakfast, drop them off at school, return home and climb back into bed.

This went on for a while until one day my mother told me she'd had enough and that I needed to get it together. I remember thinking to myself, "She's been through divorce twice with my father, how can she not understand how I'm feeling?" Sitting there I started to think that I should just quit, but I was so afraid to.

How would I pay my bills? Who would I call if I needed help? Out of nowhere one day, I heard an answer and no, I wasn't imagining it. I felt something in me say that if I walked out the door everything would be alright and that I just needed to have faith in that. Having always been true to my Virgo traits, I always tried to have a plan, a schedule, something for any major changes in my life.

Though at this moment I didn't, and the thought of taking a leap of faith was terrifying, but I did it, I got up, grabbed my keys, picked up my coat and walked out of the office, left the building, got in my car and drove away.

I was unemployed for a month and things were really tight. I wasn't very good at budgeting back then, which is why to this day I can't figure out why my husband let me handle all the finances. Some people said it was because he loved me. Let me make this clear, it's one thing to be in love and it's another thing to be in love and make poor decisions because of it.

Looking back at things, if I were him there is no way I would have let me managed the money knowing that I loved expensive items and that overspending and impulse buying are symptoms of depression, which I had a history of.

Soul SCREAM: The End Was Just The Beginning
Chapter 3

After racking up over sixty-five thousand dollars in credit card debt, building a house we couldn't afford, filing bankruptcy, and cheating, I'm sure now he will rethink letting his next wife or significant other have so much control over the finances. Last I checked he was living with young women 17 years younger than him.

Trust me I did have an issue with a woman closer in age to our three kids than him being their step parent, but I finally came to terms with it and now I say to each his own. All I have to say to her is sorry for ruining it for you because I can't see him ever relinquishing control of his paycheck to a female or anybody else for that matter, ever again, however, I could be wrong.

I'm not bragging. I'm just illustrating that when two young adults get married and have very little guidance or are willing to seek guidance in the areas of finance, marriage, and parenting, then you can expect they are going to make some huge mistakes. Huge. Believe me, we were examples of just that, but you live and you learn.

My spending habits now are a WHOLE LOT BETTER! I've learned so much being a single woman and mother. My kids can attest to that fact because I have learned to tell them and myself 'no' more than I ever did in the past.

Now I not only budget my paper money, I budget my change. You can catch me on any given day cashing in change to deposit into my savings. Yes, me! I have savings! I spent many days watching

Suze Orman's shows to help me develop the mindset needed to learn this necessary life skill. If you need any financial guidance, watch Suze Orman or pick up any one of her books. Even if you think you know everything about finances, I guarantee you that you will learn something new from her.

Oh and my divorce you ask? You want to know how that played out?

Well on the same day, I walked into court to finalize my divorce; God closed one door and opened another. I felt so relieved that day to finally be putting my marriage behind me. I take responsibility for my actions but like I said before, I was miserable in my marriage and didn't admit it to myself until after it ended.

During my marriage, my husband had bought me two pieces of jewelry I absolutely adored. The first was a 14 karat gold butterfly pendant with the wings bent up so when it was hung around my neck it looked as if it was resting on my chest with the wings up. I still miss that piece of jewelry because it just looked so elegant and beautiful. The second piece of jewelry was a puffed heart pendant encrusted in Swarovski crystals.

When he first gave it to me I didn't like it but later fell in love with how it glittered in any light. Both pieces were worn by me quite frequently and they always reminded me of how much he loved me. At least, they did before the day he moved out of our home. On that day he told me, and I quote, "You're incapable of change and you don't deserve to be loved by anyone. You'll always be the same."

These words cut me so deep I never stop repeating them in my head for close to three years following the day they were spoken to me.

Every time I looked at those two pieces of jewelry from that day forward it reminded me of what he had said to me. Those words are the reason I wrote this book. Those words are the reason I am happier today and those words are the reason that I have been able to grow in leaps and bounds mentally, spiritually and emotionally.

I used those words to help me take a harder look at myself and see what I wanted to change about me to become a better woman, mother, and overall person. Those words were meant to destroy me, but I chose to use them to build me up. That's what I taught myself to do with negative words and negative actions towards me from others.

I use that stuff like a slingshot to keep the fight in me. Always fighting to develop myself to a higher level. I got a lot of practice doing this with the way people were quick to judge and persecute me because of their opinion of how my divorce came about.

The day I walked into that courthouse to finalize my divorce I had no idea that as God closed one door, He was about to open so many others for me. Once we had gotten done in the courtroom, as I was walking out I turned back and handed my soon to be ex-husband a small jewelry box with those two pieces of jewelry inside.

I said to him, "These inspired me to look deeper so I could start healing and growing in positive ways. Take them, they belong to you. Maybe you know someone else they can inspire to change."

I felt like a weight had been lifted off of me as I held my head high, spun around on my four-inch heels and walked away with class. I was proud of myself for saying what I needed to say in a classy yet mature way in the midst of this tense day. It felt AMAZING!

In the lobby, I hugged my lawyer whom I absolutely adored and proceeded to walk to the parking garage. As I crossed the street, lo and behold my phone rang. I answered it only to discover that the company that I had just interviewed with a few days ago was calling to offer me a job! Like really?!

   I was loss for words, which was saying a lot considering I always had something to say around that period in my life. In short, I lost a husband, but gained a much-needed job in less than three hours! Truly amazing!! My world was starting to come together so fast, and I was learning so many lessons that God needed me to learn.

Although, I must admit that some of the lessons made me happy and, of course, there were others that brought me back to tears as well back then. The life I have today is more than I could have ever asked for, but getting to this point I've had to learn what feels like one too many lessons and many of them I was far overdue to learn.

Believe me, I'm still learning every second of every day and I keep myself open to learning always. I love who I've become through all of this. I'm a better mother, daughter, friend, and woman despite having made the biggest mistake of my life, having an affair. It's almost as if I'm a better person because of the affair.

Do you have doubts that a person can be truly remorseful for their actions and change? Do you think 'once a cheater always a cheater?' You wouldn't be the first to feel that way, and while in the past I would have agreed, now I know differently.

When my husband left me, he told me that I wasn't capable of change and that I would never be able to do so. His words are on the wall in my bedroom for me to see every day. I believe that God has taken these words that my ex-husband spoke to me and was able to use them to touch me and guide me in attaining the change that He wanted for me, change that I needed.

In my living room, my divorce decree is framed on the wall. Why did I put it on the wall? Because every day I look at it, I see where I was and thank God for bringing me to where I am now. I never want to forget my past. Please take note of what I'm saying here. If we forget the past, I believe we are destined to repeat it, sometimes over and over again.

Why? Because the lesson that God intended for us to learn, we didn't. Plain and simple. Sometimes instead of working through our mistakes in life, we chose to attempt to forget them to get past them. We want to forget the hurt, the pain, and the anger. However, I believe that if we work through all these emotions, then we can learn the lesson and use it to become wiser and make better life choices.

When you think you know all there is to know about someone or something, trust me, you don't. It's sad to think that the person whom you were so quick to judge is someone whom you really don't know.

Why? Because until you've walked in someone else's shoes you truly don't know them. I was with my ex- husband for fifteen years, and while I thought I knew all of him, I now know I didn't know him at all. His actions and the way he treated me then and still treats me now showed me, our kids and others around us that we didn't know him. And honestly, how could he have known me when I didn't even know myself until recently?

So, now I'm going to share with you the lessons that God has taught me, how He made me aware of the fact that I needed to learn them and how He taught them to me. I am and will be forever open to learning what I need to grow as a person through any means necessary so I can progress because I now know that progression is a choice we have to do so.

I know now that I must put effort in every day to be a better person today than I was yesterday. Simply sharing what I know now is just one more way for me to show God how grateful I am for everything that He has done for me, and I intend to show Him my appreciation forevermore.

CHAPTER {4}

LESSON 1: LEARNING TO LEARN

#

Why did I break my husband's heart? That's easy to answer because I was broken and broken people break other people. This fact I can never let myself forget. The same way hurting people hurt people. It's a fact and I'm living proof of it.

I dislike when people have a painful life experience and other people simply tell them to get over it or forget about it. I want to believe the intent of the people telling them to do this is to redirect the person's attention away from whom or what hurt them. While I understand the intent, I've discovered personally that this approach didn't work for me.

Now before you go shutting my book and putting it on a shelf to collect dust next to the other books with empty promises of self-growth that may have hit a personal chord with you, please hear me out further.

When I was a child my parents would always tell me, like parents are supposed to, what was safe and what would hurt me. Now from my parental experiences, I saw that some parents define a good child as one who when told not to do something, doesn't do it.

On the other hand, there are the kids whom you would refer to as bad. My mother, being in the field of education and child care, has always believed that the word 'bad,' when used in reference to a child, does not help to foster positive behavior or thinking so she uses 'busy' to describe 'bad' children. I myself, being a parent, understand this and use this term 'busy' as well.

When a 'busy' child is told not to do something, they may ask fifty questions as to why they shouldn't. And if they feel that your answers aren't adequate enough, then they'll go right ahead and do exactly what you asked them not to do.

Case in point – One day I was cooking and my daughter Chelsea, who was three years old at the time, asked me why the stove was red. I told her that it was hot and that she should never touch it. Sure enough, as soon as I turned my back she took her finger and touched it right to the electric burner while it was piping hot! Thankfully, she ended up with just a burnt fingertip and not her whole hand.

After I got her finger taken care of I asked her why she did it. She simply replied, "I wanted to find out for myself if it was really hot." Now at the time I wanted to kill her after hearing that response, considering she had scared me half to death, but I decided to let the incident go. I later found out that I was quite the same when I was growing up.

Chelsea felt that in order for her to learn that the stove would hurt her she needed to confirm the information I had given her for herself. Does that make her a bad child? No, it makes her a child who knew what she had been told, but who felt the need to discover for herself how hot the stove really was. Had she asked me I would have done something visually to confirm it for her in a safer manner, but what was done was done and flipping out wasn't going to heal her finger any faster.

I could have run out and bought her a new toy to take her attention away from the fact that she hurt herself considering she cried and whined all night due to her finger hurting, but I didn't. I could have taken her out for ice cream or a treat, but did I? No. I remember telling my husband, "Well she learned what she wanted to know and after dealing with the consequences I bet she'll never touch the stove again."

I was right because over the next twelve years Chelsea never touched the stove again. She doesn't even enjoy cooking even though she can, so good luck to my future son in law. Just kidding, Chelsea. So in short, my daughter got the lesson. It wasn't the way I wanted her to get it, but she got it nonetheless.

When we have painful or joyful experiences in our life we have the opportunity to learn from all of them, but the one thing I've learned is that as we get older and our emotions develop more, we have a harder time processing the emotions and it takes us longer to get the lesson or sometimes we just don't get it at all.

A five-year-old who gets in a fight with a classmate will be back playing with the same child possibly by the end of the school day. However, an adult who has a disagreement with a friend may be more likely to not speak to that friend for weeks, months or maybe even years. Believe me, I've been there and done that and received no joy from it either.

I wish we could be more like the five-year-old and be quick to forgive, learn from our mistakes, and keep moving forward, but unfortunately, most of us adults aren't like this.

As we get older we become more aware of our emotions and, therefore, are affected by them more deeply. So to try and get an adult to process a painful experience the same way, in my opinion, isn't as easy sometimes, especially depending on the situation.

What I believe a friend or family member should do is to try and help the person pick thru the painful event and find understanding as to why it occurred, what role the person themselves played in the event, and how they can learn from it going forward.

One goal in doing this is to possibly prevent themselves from having to relive it again and again through subsequent similar life situations. Now, that's not to say that if you complete all three steps that you won't go through it again, you may. Nevertheless, the goal is to learn a little more from it each time in the hopes that you will become stronger, and if you do go through it again you'll be able to handle it in a way that may be healthier for you emotionally, mentally, and physically.

I went through so many situations repeatedly before I finally learned this lesson. If I had learned this sooner, I could have saved myself a world of hurt, but isn't that what we all say? Well here's the thing, we could have, but we didn't, so there's no use in dwelling on the past. You can't change it so the best thing you can do is learn from it and keep it moving.

Many people go around saying they've learned their lesson, yet turn right around and put themselves right back in the same situations and to make it worse, sometimes with the same people. There is more to learning a lesson than knowing about it, you need to why you're being taught it.

For example, my mom and I don't always see eye to eye on some topics, like most parents and their kids. Even as an adult we can still tend to butt heads. My mom is a strong independent-thinking woman who will state her point and make sure to back it up with plenty of facts. Being a child of a different generation, I tend to disagree sometimes with her views. I used to argue back and forth with her over and over.

I mean, we could go back and forth about a certain topic about three or four times a year and the result was always the same. I usually ended up speaking to her in a disrespectful manner and then not talking to her for a few weeks or even months. My mom usually wound up feeling as though I had no respect for her because I was raised to act better than I had.

This went on for years until finally one day; I was watching Joel Osteen preach a sermon on only fighting the battles that affect your destiny and leaving the rest of them up to God. I stopped and thought to myself if she never sees agrees with me on my decisions, actions, views and topics what will happen?

The answer was nothing. Nothing at all was going to happen to me or her. So I stopped arguing with her because it was pointless. My mom is going to always be my mom and she's going to have an opinion on what I do, think, say and believe, but at the end of the day, it doesn't change who I am.

I took control of the situation by taking accountability for myself, my actions and how I was allowing them to affect me. The only person, who can change who I am, how I make my decisions and how I live, is me.

So why was I wasting so much energy trying to change my mom and her way of viewing things? Energy that I could have been using elsewhere in my life to accomplish goals and get other things done. I took control over the situation by taking control over me, my mouth and my behavior.

This is how and when God taught me the meaning of and how to honor thy mother and father, no kidding. I no longer argue, yell and scream with my mom, father or anyone else for that matter. At least, I try my hardest not to because it was taking too much energy from me.

Learning this was priceless. However, had someone told me that backing down from my parents in a discussion would make my life so much easier, I wouldn't have believed them.

Some of the lessons I was confronted with repeatedly and it took me thirty-five years to finally learn and start practicing them. Yup, you read right, thirty-five years because of my stubbornness. One reason was because I thought I knew it all in some areas of my life and because of this I wasn't able to see that there was so much more that I needed to learn.

Consider this:

#

In times of change, learners inherit the earth; while the learned find themselves beautifully equipped to deal with a world that no longer exists. – Eric Hoffer

#

I absolutely love this quote! It was first presented to me by Simon T. Bailey in his amazing book "Release Your Brilliance: The 4 Steps to Transforming Your Life and Revealing Your Genius to the World." This book, when you're ready, is a great book to further help you increase your self-esteem, set and achieve your goals in life.

Soul SCREAM: The End Was Just The Beginning
Chapter 4

This quote had such a profound influence on me that I had it on my cell phone as the background for over a year and on a wall in the house for my kids to read every day. I never understood that in order to learn something you have to be open and ready to learn until it was taught to me.

My ex-husband was the primary person to bring to my attention the fact that I was not open to learning in order to grow. I ignored what he said for years because I had lost respect for him.

Another reason was because of how he had presented it to me, and the fact that I perceived his presentation method as him judging and criticizing me, not trying to empower me. Honestly, I don't know if I was wrong or right about his intentions, but it really doesn't matter anymore, now does it? When you become open to learning, you will be able to look beyond particular actions and emotions to focus more on deciphering the lesson at hand.

The pain of losing my family and walking away from Cameron all around the same period of time was so great that I became determined to learn the lessons I needed to learn so I would never have to feel that level of pain again due to my ignorance.

Similar to how I would always say that I would never cheat, I started to tell myself that if I learned the lessons that were before me (because of this life altering event), that I would never have to go through it again. I was wrong, though. It's like when couples say to each other, "I'll never leave you; we're in this together, forever." And yup, my husband and I had said that too.

We even went as far as to have it engraved on the inside of our wedding bands. In his it read, "SHANIIKA AND 'HIS NAME' FOREVER" and in mine, it read, "'HIS NAME' AND SHANIIKA FOREVER." Because this was there on my hand every day, I really believed that we would be together, forever.

In reality, what couples should be saying as they approach the idea of marriage is, "I pray that it is in God's will for us to be together forever." No matter what we may want or plan, if He feels there is something that we must learn or that the person we're with will hinder our growth, especially with Him, then we may have to leave them to do so.

Please don't think because I'm sitting here sharing this with you that my life is easier than it was before. Life doesn't really get easier, you simply become smarter at navigating through it and mature at making better decisions as you go along. To tell you the truth, the stronger and wiser you get the greater your challenges become.

It's all worth it though because God will say to you just as the master in the parable said, "Well done, good and faithful servant; you have been faithful over a little, I will set you over much" (Matthew 25:21).

While I have excelled in some areas, I still have a lot of growth to do in others. Some days I feel like I will be working on patience for the rest of my life unless God sees fit to give me a huge learning curve and I mean a HUGE one. The point is that as you continue to read I implore you to open your spirit, mind, and heart to learning something new or looking at a lesson you already learned in a new way.

I don't expect you to finish reading this book and wake up the next morning as an expert, nor do I expect you to fully grow overnight in the areas of your life that you need to grow in. Everybody's timeframe for getting where God wants them to be is different. What I've learned and how I've grown in just five years may take someone else one or possibly two years to accomplish. It's up to you and Him to determine that, but that's beside the point.

My aim is to show you how to open up emotionally and mentally to allow for God to teach you the lessons that He has for you, and so that you can grow more in the various aspects of who you are in your life starting today, one step at a time. Unlike those who told me I was incapable of growing and becoming a better person, I'm telling you that I have faith in your ability to achieve this if you want it.

Progressing and learning are two things we should never stop doing and it's our choice to do so. Your future is what you make it and you can change its direction any second of any day. How do I know this? Because I did, and I know that if you truly want to you can too.

CHAPTER {5}

LESSON 2: GIVING IT ALL TO HIM

#

So, how do you move forward, how do you start to grow in the midst of the feeling hurt and pain, especially when you've sacrificed and lost so much?

Honestly, I had to pray and pray and when I was done, go back and pray some more. In the last five years, I have prayed more than I prayed during the whole fifteen years that I was with my ex-husband.

Looking back, though, I don't believe initially that my prayers were for the right reasons. In the beginning, I started praying, because, well, that's what everybody does when they go through some major kind of hurt and disappointment. They call on God to fix it, to heal it, and to make it better. So, I prayed to God to bring my husband back home and to bring my family back together because that was what I felt I was supposed to do.

I know now that I wasn't praying because I was declaring to God that I was going to change or become a better person. I was praying because I was terrified that the one person who had been the most stable in my life over the last fifteen years had left me. I was praying because I grew up in a home with a father, and I wanted my kids to have the same experience.

Even though my parents had gotten divorced when I was in my early twenties and then again in my late twenties, I still attributed my happy childhood to the fact that my father was there when I was younger and I wanted my children to have that. I prayed because my whole life had been set up and I had financial security provided by husband's career and employment.

I prayed because my daughter's biological father didn't have much to do with her and my husband was the only man that she truly had formed a strong relationship with and knew as "Dad." I prayed because the world that I had known for so long, of being with my husband was changing, and change with no plan or knowledge of possible outcomes scared the hell out of me.

Change had always been something that scared me, even as a child, but even more so as an adult. I had always been an emotional and very dramatic child, as my parents would say and now I was an adult of the same accord.

Back then I thought my praying was for the right reasons. It was sincere, but it wasn't for the reasons that I now know God would support as valid enough to put my family back together. I believe that He heard my prayers but could see in my heart that the two weren't exactly lining up. I wanted my family, but I was still truly in love with another man.

I truly do believe that there were things that I still needed to learn in order to grow as a person and I wouldn't have been able to do so with either of these men in my life at that time. It was time for me to focus on me.

Now five years later I realize that the greatest blessing that God gave me was not sending my husband back to me and not allowing me to run back to Cameron.

Why would I believe this? Well for starters, even though I was praying and saying the things that most people would say in my situation, I can see now that had my husband returned, the praying would have stopped. I would have become more focused on trying to be whomever I needed to be to please him and get his forgiveness. I never would have experienced the pain which is what I used to facilitate the start of my spiritual development and personal growth.

The thing is, when we're happy and/or comfortable, some of us don't seek God or His guidance as hard. When our world is going what we consider "perfectly", then we might take a minute to throw Him a thank you, like a bone to a dog and continue living in our happy little moments.

But let tragedy or something painful come our way, the first thing we do is turn to Him and then we want to stay wrapped up in His strong arms and in His loving voice, for however long we need in order to get through it. As soon as we get through it or He fixes it, we stop turning to Him as much and it's back to living our life how we want.

When things feel good again, we don't feel the need to seek Him as diligently as we did when we were hurting. Now before I continue on this topic let me say that I know there are some people reading this saying to them self, "I don't do that." Don't forget the last word of that statement, "anymore". We all started out at the bottom and worked our way up. Maybe you don't, maybe you stay tuned into God 24/7 no matter what the situation and I'm proud of you because it's not easy progressing to that level of action backed by faith.

But I ask you politely, please don't judge the rest of us who still have challenges in this area and are learning this lesson still. Before you go saying to yourself, "I don't need this lesson but I'm gonna call my girl Martia and tell her to read this because she needs this more than me with her situation", slow your role.

Your girl or guy friend may need it more but right now, at this moment, I want the person reading this book to be a little more selfish and focus just on yourself first. If you want to suggest the book to them that's fine but what I don't want you to do is be focused on anyone else's life or issues but your own right now.

Sound selfish? Yup, it does, because it is. Let your girlfriend or guy friend, whoever it is, wonder in confusion a little longer and wait. Chances are if they've been in a certain situation for a while, they're not changing it in the next couples of hours, days or week anyway. I want you to focus on you more while you're reading this book and you'll understand why when you're done.

Now back to my story and the point, I believe that God wanted me to learn that He must be sought all the time in everything we do. Big things and little things, it doesn't matter. I started thanking Him for getting me out the door on time for work each day or making all the street lights turn green when I'm running late headed somewhere.

Good or bad, big or small, we must give credit to Him and thanks to Him for all of it and through all of it. So I reiterate again, that at that time in my life had He sent my ex-husband or Cameron back, I would have become so fixated on him that I would've forgotten about God and I wouldn't have grown.

As much as it pained me to come to this realization, once I did, it made perfect sense and by this time, I could admit I used to be a very mentally and emotionally weak woman back then. With my ex leaving, I sought a new different relationship with God. In that new relationship, I've grown in ways I could never have imagined or planned. I've been loved more than I've ever been loved and I've matured into an amazing woman whom I sincerely love and value.

When my ex first left you would have thought that the first thing I'd have done would be to never contact Cameron again, however, my heart wanted what it wanted and it was still Cameron. See, I'd been friends with him since high school, so I still felt like I could maintain the friendship without the physical attraction, a platonic friendship of sorts.

Boy was I wrong; I couldn't stop the physical and emotional attraction no matter how hard I tried. It took me a couple months to realize that I was going to have the same problem with Cam that I would have had with my husband coming back; I would have been more focused on pleasing Cam than myself.

When I was married, during the last year of the marriage, my husband and I had a serious lack of intimacy and we didn't make time to spend with one another. I suggested that we should schedule our time together, whether it be a date night or nights for us to enjoy each other's company at home.

Like I stated previously, he told me that he didn't want to do that, that he felt that we shouldn't have to schedule time together, that our time together and intimacy should just come naturally.

After watching a talk show where husbands and wives had suffered through the same exact situation and had come up with several different scenarios in order to overcome it, I disagreed. Times were changing and I felt that we needed to change as well. My ex was more of a traditionalist, and he just felt that the puzzle pieces should fall into place over time, that we shouldn't have to sit down and focus to put them back in. So we didn't.

We went to therapy, and after the therapist spoke to each of us individually she told us to separate. She felt that it would be best that we separate because we weren't on the same page.

Now, she didn't tell us what the other one had said to make her feel that way, and she didn't share with us why she was pushing us in that direction, but I believe that was the first knife in the broken heart of our marriage.

I now realize that there are therapists out there who actually tell people to separate for financial gain. Counseling a husband and wife together can be billed as one session, but counseling a husband and wife separately, well, that's two claims which equals twice the income. So, I don't know if that was truly her intention, but I've always questioned in my mind if I was told to separate from my husband for her financial gain. It is a very troubling thought as I think about it five years later.

Not all therapists are like this, I've had some great ones that are spiritually based and promote working it out together, but the reality is there are two sides to a coin and everyone should remember this.

I'm just saying, in the future if I were going to seek a licensed marriage counselor or therapist I would prefer to seek advice from one who has a Christian foundation before I seek advice from someone who does not. I mean let's keep it real, did you go through the phonebook to find someone to marry you? So why would you seek help to keep your marriage from the phonebook? I'm just saying, put a little more work into deciding to whom you turn to for help in your marriage and again, this is just my personal opinion.

With the intimacy and communication suffering in my marriage, I reached out to Cameron my friend because I had always had more male friends as a kid. I just clicked better with men but now as an adult, I now understand why this was wrong.

I reached out to my friend but I was no longer a girl and he a boy, we were adults and whether I like it or realized it the dynamics of relationship would never be able to be platonic, ever again. So, I continued to talk to him when I was down.

I thought that when things got to a low point with my husband and I didn't feel loved, God sent this man into my life to love me because that's what I needed and wanted.

What I later realized was that even if I was meant to be with Cam, God would never have sent him to me at this point in my life. How could I think that He would send me love like this with all the chaos in my life at that time and I while I was still under a vow to my husband? God would never do that.

I had fought for fifteen years to keep my relationship going with my ex. Early on we separated, at least, three times, one of which was when the twins were one years old and he filed for emergency custody. So, the twins' first Easter, I wasn't with them, and that really hurt.

A year, later on, Mother's Day, he called me up and asked me if I wanted to do something for the day. He took me and the kids out to the park for the day, for a picnic in the park. I remember lying on the blanket, staring up at the clouds, saying to myself, "I can get this right, I can fix this." From that day forward, I dedicated everything that I had to that relationship.

Somewhere in there, I was no longer myself, I truly became just a mother and his spouse. The person that I was before I met him and had the kids, I let go of because I didn't think I could keep all of these facets of who I was and still please my husband. I went to the extreme to be the best mother and best spouse that I could.

The problem was, over many years, it was like running a race, you can't keep running at the same pace the entire race, you get tired and worn out, and you have to stop, breathe and rest, or stop and just walk at a slower pace, but I didn't.

I kept on running, and here I was at year fifteen of our relationship and marriage, tired and exhausted from trying to please him, my family, his family, our kids and everyone around me in general. I believe that not only was I tired, but that I literally died from exhaustion, and in dying I mean to say that a part of me died.

Soul SCREAM: The End Was Just The Beginning
Chapter 5

My morals and values of who I was in the beginning no longer existed. I had always prided myself on the fact that I never cheated at all during my lifetime and on the fact that I wouldn't, since I was a child who saw the effects of my father's extramarital relationships on my home life and mother. However, I turned around and did exactly what he'd done. The worst part is that I tried to justify it because I loved Cameron deeply and he loved me.

The truth is it wasn't right for me to be with Cam at that time and Cam deserved a woman who didn't have all the confusion and chaos that I had in my life. I mean let's be honest he wasn't married I was and Cameron wasn't the kind of man that went around looking for married woman to cheat with. I believe it was just because it was me and our history that he made exceptions to the rules for me truly not knowing that he was being pulled into my messy life. I mean, after all, I had told him my marriage was pretty much over.

So, after my husband moved out and the divorce was in the works I decided it best to let Cam go and I had no one.

I was so lonely. I was depressed, even getting out of the bed in the morning to get the kids ready for school became the hardest feat in my day. I wasn't sure how I was going to get through it, and every time ex came to the house to get the children I felt more lost and alone each time.

I remember one snowy day, it was in the evening about three months after my ex had moved out, a snowstorm had hit, and he had picked up the kids and they were with him at his new home. He called me on my phone and asked me if I was okay, I told him no.

He said to me that when he was going through a really troubling period after he had found out about the affair that he also had a very hard time. He told me that he had to set the timer on his phone to go off every two hours and that every two hours he would stop and pray because that was the only way that he was going to get through it. He suggested that I do the same.

This phone call was totally expected and the man on the other end was not the man whom I had been arguing with and going back and forth with since he found out about the affair. This man on the phone was the man who I had fell in love with and married. He had finally resurfaced and was now on the phone with me being nice and cordial and talking to me like the friends we were before we started dating years ago. This guy surely had been missed of late.

We sat on the phone and talked like old friends for about an hour and a half while he shoveled the driveway in front of his home. We just talked about stuff, nothing in particular. The one thing we never had a problem doing was talking. Sometimes I think that we knew how to be better friends than we knew how to be husband and wife. I think that's part of growing up, honestly.

Soul SCREAM: The End Was Just The Beginning
Chapter 5

As the phone call was ending, he told me that he just wanted to call and check in on me to make sure I was okay, because he could see I was having a hard time when he picked up the kids. I told him thank you, and even though I didn't want the conversation to end we hung up the phone. That was the very last conversation I had with my friend. The conversations to follow over the next four years would be filled with anger, pain, hatred, and any other negative emotions that could be felt from our divorce.

Sometimes I believe that on that day he realized that the part of him which had always been my friend and spouse over the years was dying, the person who had co-existed with me for so long was about to cease to exist very shortly, and this phone call was his goodbye phone call to me. I remember it like it was yesterday, lying in our bed of fifteen years in the master bedroom on the phone with him on that snowy night.

In the year following, the things that I did to try and get him back in our home were childish and yielded no results. See, I thought that I could change physically and that this would bring my husband back. So I started watching what I ate, losing weight, and exercising. I made sure that if I ever had to be in his presence that I had on makeup and was absolutely stunning. But he didn't come back.

One time I showed up at co-parenting therapy, where we should have been learning to work together as a team, and I came in heels and cute dresses and I thought I was going to appeal to him physically and sexually, but it didn't work. I tried being nice to him and being cordial, being calm, acting as if nothing happened, but he didn't come back.

Then I tried being the jealous angry woman who was mad, but he didn't come back. I tried making up stories about other women who wanted him, even if he didn't want them (though I don't think I was really making them up, I really did see other women who wanted to be with him), but it didn't change anything.

In the months to follow, I used to drive by his house late at night on my way home and stare at his window just wondering what he or the kids were doing. In that house: Was there another woman, had he already started something physically, mentally, or emotionally with another woman?

My kids came home and were telling me about the woman that he worked with and the messages that she would send on his phone and the phone calls that they would have; they felt that Dad had already started another relationship, and that killed me even more, knowing that somebody else was comforting him. Somebody else was taking the pain in his heart and helping him. The person who would normally do that for me was Cam, so it was another harsh reminder that I didn't have anybody.

After a year of playing all these games, trying to get him back and manipulate him into coming home, I finally stopped. I realized that there was nothing that I could do that would bring this man back and that I only wanted him because I couldn't have him. I just couldn't register the thought and wrap my head around the idea that it was over and that he was gone; the person that I knew was gone.

As crazy as it sounds, I had a memorial service for him and the end of our marriage. I sat and went through all the pictures that he and I had of the life that we had shared over the years and then I wrote out what sounded like an obituary. In it, I recounted all the years that we were happy and the things that we did before we had the boys, the car rides we used to go on, the fun stuff we did, and even the things we did after the kids were born. I said goodbye to my husband and the concept of married life.

For the next couple of months, I mourned. That was the only way that I was going to get over losing all that I had lost. This was the only concept that I could wrap my brain around, the fact that it was all dead, it was all gone. I even went on the internet and looked up the five stages of grief and proceeded to go through them.

Then after I was done mourning the loss of him I mourned the loss of Cameron. Regardless of what had happened, I really loved him and in order for me to move forward to focus on me so I could grow, I had to let them both go. Once I had gone through all of this, it was then that I reached out even more to God.

Things started to become a little bit different. I started to see and learn things that I hadn't seen before. I started to take a note of the people that I had around me, and while I had some great people in my life over the years, God started to show me that some of these people were not helping me grow and become the woman that I was supposed to be. They were enabling a lot of my bad behaviors, not helping me step up to the plate to mature and take responsibility for my decisions and actions which affected my life.

As He revealed these people to me one-by-one I let them go. I walked away from them, and I realized that I hadn't kept them necessarily because they were really good friends, I kept them because I had a problem with change. Like I said before, for me change was a scary thing, especially not knowing what was coming next. My whole life I had always planned out everything that I wanted to do.

My children weren't planned, but I knew if I had unprotected sex that I was going to get pregnant. In my head, technically, I HAD planned knowing that this could happen, so it never scared me because one of my morals when I became an adult was to never be in a relationship with someone that I couldn't see myself raising a child with.

I held true to that, and I believe that's why I have children by two really good men. They're not perfect, but compared to some other men out here, they were way better providers and fathers than most. Regardless of what we've been through, I won't take that from them and I will give credit where credit is due.

As I started to change the people in my world, I started to see my world change. I pulled away from people who fostered negative behaviors in me. I pulled away from people who encouraged me to argue with my ex-husband and fight back on everything he said. I fostered stronger relationships with the people whom I shared peace since this is now what I also desired.

Those who encouraged me not to fight, who taught me that life didn't have to be a war 24/7, these people helped me understand who I was and who I wanted to be. Because they were there for me during the hardest time, I started to trust them. I realized that, being who I am, I needed to have these people around me to help me grow. I didn't need to be around people who, when I did something wrong, didn't say anything for fear of losing me as a friend.

I needed to be around people who were more concerned with my well-being than with what I thought of them or our friendship. They truly loved me, and because they truly loved me they spoke up because they wanted me to be the best me that I could become.

They didn't care if it meant that I was going to pull away, they just wanted me to be a better and happier person. These people truly love me and these people are still in my life today, and I thank God every day that they are and that He's given them the strength to show me where I need to grow and tell me when I'm wrong.

He has softened my heart to show me that I don't know everything and I won't know everything I need to know, but that I can trust he will put the right people in my life to teach me every lesson that I need to know. When I become stubborn or hardened, as long as I keep His Word on my mind, on my lips, and in my heart, I'll be open to receiving all the lessons that He has for me to learn.

So, I guess if I have to sum it all up, how did I survive after losing my husband and having to walk away from Cameron? It was by continuing to read the Word and growing closer to God. In doing so, He started to put the puzzle pieces into place piece by piece. I won't discredit God by saying that they fell into place because I truly believe that they didn't fall. He strategically placed each piece in place the more I read, sought understanding and applied my understanding of His Word to my life.

Living His Word wasn't easy because I saw many people out there in the world who weren't living by His Word and they seemed so much happier than I was. There was a period that I thought I could do that and be happy again, but when I did, I realized that it was not a true happiness, it was a physical or material happiness; it was happiness here in the human world, one wherein your spirit you're not truly whole and happy.

I've always heard people say "living of the flesh," now I understand what they mean by it. Living according to the desires of the flesh drive us away from the path that God knows we should be on. When we choose to live our life the way that we see others live theirs and try to justify it, it doesn't feel good if we know that God wants more for us.

Most women would be praying for someone, and I won't say that I didn't, because I did, but I wasn't ready for a relationship and I knew it. What I realized was that once I turned my focus onto God and the ways of His Son, Christ, He didn't just want me to be with anyone, but He wanted me to be with someone special.

Someone who wouldn't just come in and make me happy physically or even emotionally, but someone whose spirit would be able to intertwine with my own and make me not only a better person but a better Christian. He wanted me to be with someone who will, when I drop the ball and stop reading the Word or stray from following 'His ways,' step in, grab my hand, and lovingly guide me back to Him, as I would do the same for them.

Sometimes in not getting what you ask for He gives you what you need. It's hard for us to see this because we have a predefined human concept of what we need here in the physical, but what we fail to understand is that He deals in the spiritual and the physical. He's not just providing one side of what we need; He's providing all of what we need.

I believe that I have not been able to find anyone that truly makes me happy because He wants me to be completely happy and whole before I do.

Although at times I am terribly lonely, I know I'm really not alone. I love to reminisce about my marriage and how great it was at times and how loving we were towards each other. I also think about how great I used to feel about myself when I was with Cameron, how he used to treat me so great, and value me so highly. As crazy as it sounds both of these men have helped me better understand what I am striving for in my next relationship and how I will make it better.

I never thought that I would hear myself say, "I'm glad my ex-husband left." I believe that in allowing him to leave, God still knew what He was doing for me. I'm sure he was doing something for him too, but that's his trial and tribulation that he'll have to talk to God on. For me, it hurt when he left, but in him being gone I've become ten times the person and woman that I ever would have been had he remained.

If he had stayed, I would have lost my focus and I wouldn't have changed, but now that I have changed the pain, the tears, the anger, the bitterness, and the resentment, they're all gone. I tried to cry a month ago and I couldn't even get a tear to come out. How amazing He is to have taken tears that I cried for so long and now not even let them fall.

Surviving this period to get to where I am now wasn't easy; however, it was worth it. While I have some regrets, I have very few. I love who I am today, I love who I've become. If there's a chance that I wouldn't have become this woman had he stayed, then I'm glad he's gone. I don't regret my life decisions, but I do regret the pain my decisions caused.

Some people will never quite understand that, but for those of you who do, stay your course. Keep your Bible with you every day and read His Word. Listen to music that sings His praises. Surround yourself with Him and praise Him every day. For some people, going to church once a week is enough to recharge their soul and keep them on His path and keep them focused on Him, but what I've found out about me is that I need time with Him every day; whenever I can fit praise in through my music I do.

I try to remember to make the first song of the day on the way to work each morning "Praise to Him," and I have voluntarily made listening to this song part of my routine out of respect and love for Him. I wake up, and while I'm getting dressed I try to listen to sermons by Joyce Meyer, Joel Osteen, Creflo Dollar, Apostle Raymond Stansbury and many others.

This is what I call my coffee in the morning. This is what charges me up and gets me ready to go out into the world. It helps me to not forget who I am and remember to stay on my path during the day.

While I'm at work, I listen to more sermons and more music by various new pastors and artists. In between all of this, I still listen to other genres of music and watch other movies, I still love my rap and hip hop, but I know now that in order for me to stay on my predestined path I need Him in my everyday in some way.

If you were to visit my home, you would turn to the left once you walked through the front door and you would see framed my divorce decree still. Many people thought this was crazy until I explain it to them. I hang that on my wall so that every day I can see who I used to be, and who I no longer want to be, seeing it reminds me of where I don't want to go. It encourages me to stay on the path, to make better choices, to be the bigger person, and to continue to grow. Some people say that we need to get over stuff and forget it, but that's not true, we need to forgive, "and be kind to one another, tenderhearted, forgiving one another more than anything else.

But we must always remember, because in remembering there's opportunity for growth. The expression, "Forgive and Forget" is not actually a helpful antidote to live by. It is in remembering that we learn, lest we fall into the same bad behavior. In turn, we must also learn from the mistakes of those who have sinned against us.

In forgiveness, there's opportunity for healing, and those two things are necessary for us to evolve as people, but if we forget our mistakes and forget our poor decisions and actions, then we are destined to repeat them again until we get the lesson that was there from the time before.

Up until my divorce, everything in my life was planned out. Everything ran by a schedule, by a system.

The crazy thing is, once I found God and He could hear me, the system went out the window and the schedule ceased to exist. I no longer know what's coming tomorrow or the day after. I no longer know what the plan is. Sometimes I have none. The only thing I know is that He will give me everything I need and take me where I need to go and I trust Him to do so.

I now walk in more faith than I ever had in the past, and change doesn't scare me anymore, I welcome it. It's amazing what

He can do for you, and how He can awaken you unto a new self when you let Him. People say they're alone because they don't feel God or hear God, but the truth is, Christ is with us all of the time, every day, every second, every minute.

Even the people on the street, God is with them and Christ is with them. Always. In order for us to feel Him, in order for us to hear Him, we have to be open to it. Once you open your heart, your mind, and your soul to Him, the one thing I promise you is that you will never feel alone again.

One morning I discovered Joyce Meyer while flipping through the television channels and instantly identified with the sermon she was preaching. On this particular morning, she shared a story written by Larry Harp in the form of a letter to the reader.

I share this with you because I don't think I can express what he wrote any better. After you read it I ask that you read it again. Then go online to my site and print it out and hang it somewhere so that you will see it every day. Even if you don't read it just glancing at it each day will help you remember what is written and help to keep you on your path of healing and progress.

Sometimes just knowing that we need to heal isn't enough. We need to surround ourselves with healing and work on it every second of every day. Knowing when to let go and move forward is the best lesson I've learned so far.

#

"Leaving the City of Regret" by Larry Harp

I had not really planned on taking a trip this time of year, and yet I found myself packing rather hurriedly. This trip was going to be unpleasant and I knew in advance that no real good would come of it. I'm talking about my annual "Guilt Trip."

I got tickets to fly there on Wish I Had airlines. It was an extremely short flight. I got my baggage, which I could not check. I chose to carry it myself all the way. It was weighted down with a thousand memories of what might have been. No one greeted me as I entered the terminal to the Regret City International Airport. I say international because people from all over the world come to this dismal town.

As I checked into the Last Resort Hotel, I noticed that they would be hosting the year's most important event, the Annual Pity Party. I wasn't going to miss that great social occasion. Many of the town's' leading citizens would be there.

First, there would be the Done family, you know, Should Have, Would Have and Could Have. Then came the I Had family. You probably know ol' Wish and his clan. Of course, the Opportunities would be present, Missed and Lost. The biggest family would be the Yesterday's. There are far too many of them to count, but each one would have a very sad story to share.

Soul SCREAM: The End Was Just The Beginning
Chapter 5

Then Shattered Dreams would surely make an appearance. And It's Their Fault would regale us with stories (excuses) about how things had failed in his life, and each story would be loudly applauded by Don't Blame Me and I Couldn't Help It.

Well, to make a long story short, I went to this depressing party knowing that there would be no real benefit in doing so. And, as usual, I became very depressed. But as I thought about all of the stories of failures brought back from the past, it occurred to me that all of this trip and subsequent "pity party" could be cancelled by ME! I started to truly realize that I did not have to be there. I didn't have to be depressed. One thing kept going through my mind, I CAN'T CHANGE YESTERDAY, BUT I DO HAVE THE POWER TO MAKE TODAY A WONDERFUL DAY.

I can be happy, joyous, fulfilled, encouraged, as well as encouraging. Knowing this, I left the City of Regret immediately and left no forwarding address. Am I sorry for mistakes I've made in the past? YES! But there is no physical way to undo them.

So, if you're planning a trip back to the City of Regret, please cancel all your reservations now. Instead, take a trip to a place called, Starting Again. I liked it so much that I have now taken up permanent residence there. My neighbors, the I Forgive Myselfs and the New Starts are so very helpful.

By the way, you don't have to carry around heavy baggage, because the load is lifted from your shoulders upon arrival. God bless you in finding this great town. If you can find it -- it's in your own heart -- please look me up. I live on I Can Do It Street.

CHAPTER {6}

LESSON 3: A BLESSING MAY COME IN NOT GETTING WHAT YOU DESIRE

#

When I first separated from my husband, I prayed repeatedly for understanding and for our marriage to be saved. No matter how hard I prayed, it still came to a close with him walking out the door that momentous day. Initially, I didn't understand it; I saw it as him abandoning me. However, what I was unable to see, because my eyes had not yet been opened, was that in fact he was walking away from me.

Now, through the hurt of him leaving me, my eyes and my heart were about to be opened to God and to Christ, who had been standing there the whole time with me, ready to guide me, ready to help me grow, and ready to make me into the woman he wanted me to be in His eyes.

Growing up, all I ever wanted was to get what I wanted. I remember dating my now ex-husband and what he used to say to me. He used to tell me that no matter how much I wanted something, if he didn't think that it was right, he wouldn't give it to me.

Soul SCREAM: The End Was Just The Beginning
Chapter 6

He was the first man to say 'no' to me and the first man to stand his ground on what he believed to be right or wrong. He taught me so much by the fact that he would not feed into my childish behavior and actions by just giving me what I wanted. That's one reason why I think I clung so tightly to him in the beginning.

I was the baby girl in my family, so I had always been able to manipulate people in order to get what I wanted. I would say sweet things to my father to get him to do what I wanted, or I would run around and do whatever my mother needed done so that I could get money from her so that I could go out and buy the different things that I wanted.

In the end, all I ever learned from these experiences was that if I wanted something that I could have it, and that no one could tell me no, because I would find someone who would tell me yes. When I was younger all of this made sense, but as I started to get older I started to realize that you can't live your life that way.

Having people give you all that you want and desire is not good. It doesn't allow you to strengthen yourself, to grow, or to learn. You stay who you are and you stay where you are because you have no desire to leave, because life remains easy, comfortable. Everything flows effortlessly with neither conflicts nor issues.

Instead, we have to understand that the word 'No' is a good word. Beginning from childhood, most people associate it as a bad word because they want a Popsicle or they want candy and their parents simply says no. The truth is, that 'no' is a good word because they may not need that Popsicle, candy, or whatever else it is they desire may not be good for them. So when someone says no, what we should be doing is looking at why they are saying no.

Now this is very important because in almost every parenting book I read while raising my kids it clearly stated that if you tell a child no and if they ask "Why?" you should not respond with, "Because I said so." You should respond with a reason as to why you chose to say no.

The validity of your reason, may not seem reasonable to the child, but at the very least the child will have a reason and they will be able decipher that reason over time instead of being left to merely guess the reason.

As an adult, to have someone say no makes you realize that there are just some things that you are not going to get period.

Some things just aren't going to go the way that you want them to. Therefore, you're going to have to find out why you are getting that 'no' so you can change your path.

You are going to have to change your thought process, and possibly change your heart, in order to understand why you've gotten that no. And even though you've changed these things it doesn't guarantee that you will get a yes from the person who gave you the no initially, or even from another individual. What it will guarantee is that you will learn something from that no, and it will assist you in deciphering as to why you got it, and that is a very important thing.

In order to learn, we have to be open to learning. But if someone says no and you run around trying to find a yes, you're not opening yourself to learning why you got the no, and therefore you're not opening yourself to growing.

We must dig deeper. It is so important in who we are and in who we are to become for us to dig deeper. To just accept the things on a surface level is never enough. It's like saying: "I've gone to high school, I've finished college, I've got my master's degree, and I've got my doctorate. I'm finished. I have no more desire to learn anything else in my field. I have finished the top level of education that has been proclaimed by man, and that means that I am finished learning in this field." That is never true though.

True professionals who long to thrive at their field and become the best will continuously learn. Even after getting a doctoral degree, those who want to continue to succeed will attend seminars, read books, read articles, and do more research. A medical doctor who does not take the extra steps to learn new techniques and new ways of thinking and new ways of treatment will stop treating people effectively and efficiently at some point in time.

Consider again the quote by Eric Hoffer: "In times of change learners inherit the earth; while the learned find themselves beautifully equipped to deal with a world that no longer exists." We see that this is true because those who are learners will evolve along with the world, as well as contribute to its continued evolution.

So, the next time you get a no, realy think about why you received it. Think about if you could have done something differently to receive a yes. The fact of the matter is, in order to understand all of this you have got to be open to digging deeper. There is no other way of being able to do these things and see the lessons that are right before your eyes.

God gave us the Bible. We can sit and read it ten times over. We can memorize the verses from front to back, but unless we dig deeper and try to find the true meaning of the words and events that are in there, the book is no good to us, it will remain just that, a book of words.

When He gave it to us, He meant for us to truly try to understand His intention behind it, to read a verse and go back and see what that verse means to us in our lives today, and what it meant at the time that it was written. Our lives are like the Bible.

Don't just live your life concerned simply with your happiness, material items or people and think that you are going to be fulfilled; I can tell you that you're not. There is so much more to life than the emotions we experience. You can have the house, the car, the six digit paycheck, the perfect spouse, and still not be fulfilled. We must be living the Word in order for Him to enter us and complete us. I had to learn the hard way that there is no other way for this to be done.

True inner happiness is something we have to dig and sometimes fight for, and if we're not willing to dig the dirt from the hole to get to the source of truth of what we need to attain it, then we'll never truly find it. I feel bad for people when I hear them say: "My life is so easy, it just flows; I have no stress." Can you truly have a non-stressful life, easy life, without God? No.

What you're living is a façade. It looks that way because you allow it to look that way, but if you dig a little deeper within yourself, you'll know there are questions that need to be answered about you, your life, and the people around you.

You may not be accountable now and those duties may not become due soon, but eventually they will become due. I urge you to take a vow to dig deeper into your own life, the people that you surround yourself with, the place that you live, the person that you love, the relationship that you have with your children, and into your family on a whole.

Dig deeper.

Pick up the Bible. Try to decipher these people and their actions because it is only then that you will pull God out of each of these things and have a better understanding of yourself, your life, and them. He is everywhere and He is not going anywhere, but you must open up your mind and humble yourself in order to see and feel Him to hear what He wants from you.

This is a choice that I made wholeheartedly. It wasn't easy. Having my husband tell me no and tell me that he didn't want to be with me, and, on top of that, show me the person that he had chosen to be with, allowed me to grow to another level of understanding that made me willingly want to create an everlasting bond between myself, the Father, Christ, and the Holy Spirit.

When my daughter came home and told me that she had spent her first weekend with the young woman that my ex had been living with for a year I wanted to cry, but for some reason the tears just wouldn't come. I went to bed that night and I prayed to God because I couldn't understand why I had cried so much over the past two years and for so long, and now, when I thought that I would be the most hurt, I could not muster a single tear to fall down my face.

They welled up in my eyes, but they never fell. Why not? I prayed to God for answers. The only answer I received was that He needed me to dig deeper. He needed me to have a deeper understanding of why I did not react the way that I did. What He taught me was that the things that I choose to stress over in life are things of the world, and if I truly can give Him my heart and trust Him with my entire being, then He would see to it that I would never cry again about something or someone that He did not want me to shed a tear over.

It was in that moment that I realized that in my ex's actions lay exactly what I needed in order to grow, to humble myself, and open myself up to another level of spiritual understanding. And I did. This is how I knew that I was ready to take an even closer step into the person that He wanted me to become. Choose to dig deeper, people. What you may find may be the greatest blessing that you are to ever attain, or just one of the many blessings that are to come to you.

CHAPTER {7}

LESSON 4: DETERMINING WHO YOU'RE DESTINED TO BE AND PURSUING IT

#

For years throughout my life, I jumped around with deciding who I wanted to be and wanted to become. All I could ever think about was the career I wanted to have, how many children I wanted, and what kind of man I wanted to be married to.

What I now realize is that our lives are so much deeper than what we are able to see here in the world. While, yes, we all want to be successful, to make a certain amount of money, and to have beautiful children and a loving spouse, there are other things that play a major role in who we are and who we are to become.

When I was younger, at lunch time, if I saw a child without lunch I would offer them part of my sandwich or part of my snacks. In all honesty, I did it partially because I didn't like the sandwiches that my parents used to pack, which were always wheat bread and hard salami.

However, I also did it because I couldn't fathom sitting there eating my sandwich and watching another child not have one. I remember being like this from the time I was in first grade, and I remember people simply saying, "You're weak. You're weak. You just give in to people and you give to people who don't deserve it." But in my head everyone deserved it. Even to the worst people in the world (i.e., the kid who pushed me on the playground), I would still offer part of my sandwich if he or she forgot their lunch at home.

As I got older, some people would say that this characteristic of mine got worse, but it didn't really get worse, I just became more giving without thinking about the consequences to myself. It wasn't uncommon for me to take the last twenty dollars I had in my bank account and give it to somebody who needed it. Granted, I did have parents whom I could always call up and ask for money if I needed it, but that wasn't the reason, I didn't think about that.

I just thought to myself, "This person needs something and I have it." But at the time, I looked at my mom to replace what I had given away. I remember being in my thirties after my husband left and still encompassing this habit of giving without thinking of the consequences.

My mother turned to me one day and said to me, "I'm going to give you this money, but I'm going to need you to stop giving the shirt off your back to other people because I cannot continue to keep putting it back on you."

When she said that it really hit home, it was a very profound statement for me because that was exactly what I'd been doing. I was literally taking what I had and giving to others before taking care of myself and before taking care of my children.

Soul SCREAM: The End Was Just The Beginning
Chapter 7

I felt like God had given me a helping and giving spirit so my purpose on earth was to help people. I had always known this, but what I didn't realize was that maybe what He was trying to show me was that, yes, you are supposed to help people, but there's a proper way for you to do it so you don't create hardships for yourself.

I realize now that that God would not want me to give to the extent of not being able to provide for my family, my children, and for myself. "If anyone does not provide for his relatives, and especially for his own family, he has disowned the faith and is worse than an unbeliever" (1Timothy 5:8).

So as I started to learn more, especially after becoming financially independent following the divorce, I had to learn how to budget my paycheck, my child support, and initially my alimony. After the alimony had ended, I had to learn how to budget the child support and my paycheck. The more I read the Word in the Bible and the more I strengthened my relationship with God, what He showed me was that in the past I was helping, but I wasn't helping in the way that I should've been helping.

What I should have been doing was taking note of why people did not have what they needed. Anne Isabella Ritchie famously spurred the proverb: "Give a man a fish and you will feed him for a day; show him how to catch a fish and you feed him for a lifetime." It's true, and had I been reading the Word more in the beginning, I would have learned that God wanted me to teach people how to fish and not just give them the fish.

On the surface it seems harsh, but God is simply teaching us that He wants us all to make full use of our abilities to care for ourselves. It is so funny because I have thought of these words so many times, even repeated them, and yet every day that I was living my life, I was living it in the opposite way. So, now that I've learned this lesson, I no longer give what I cannot afford to give. I take care for myself, my children and my home first and foremost.

If I can afford to give, I give. I no longer feel bad if I can't do something for someone, because I clearly tell them straight out, "I will do what I can do and what I can't do I won't do." This is not to say that I neglect my family for the sake of others, or that I curtail giving to others under the disguise of caring for my family. I still try to live my life comfortably, but at the same time living within a means that allows me to help other people.

I could go out and buy shoes, clothes, or anything I wanted; I could spend a lot of money on my car and other material items, but for me these things are not important. There used to be a time when I thought that if I had those material items that I would be happy, I would be fulfilled, but I wasn't. Now I'm learning why, because those material items do not fulfill me. They don't define who I am nor my inner happiness.

I do believe some day that I will get to a point where I will have nice things or I will have the choice to purchase things nicer than what I have, and when I reach that point (if I choose to purchase those things) I won't look at them as "I want a better car, or I need a more expensive house," I will look at them as, "God has given me the ability to bless myself with a nicer home," or "He has told me that I have earned a nicer car now." Point being, I do not want to take of those things until He tells me that I am worthy, until I have the proper virtue to be able to keep them in their proper place below God.

Yes, I work hard every day like everyone else, and, yes, I am fulfilled by the job that I do, but unlike some people who feel that they have earned those things, I don't feel that I have, because it is not just about earning them in the world, it's about earning them in spirit and in God's work. And I don't feel that I've done enough of God's work to warrant living that lifestyle, or having these things just yet, but I know that I will.

I simply need to continue to stay on the track that I am on, which leads me toward becoming who I'm supposed to be, which allows me to help the people that I'm meant to help, and which guides me to the people who are lost so that I can lead them back to Him. I am here as a conduit of God's Love and grace so that He can provide knowledge to those who have humbled themselves and who are opened to listening and learning.

When I have done this, I know my day will come when God will give me the approval to have these things. I wait patiently because I've had them before on my own accord, on my own time and I lost them because I became so wound up in getting them and having them and having others see that I had them, that I truly could not see the value and the fact that He had given them to me; I had not really attained them myself.

So now I wait, patiently, and I am glad to wait with a smile on my face and continue to do His work and to continue to be a living example of what He wants for all of us.

My life isn't easy, but it's not hard either, nor do I want it to be. It is not always stress free and it is not always happy, but that's okay because I know that in all of the things of my life God is teaching me. And because my eyes and spirit are now open, I'm able to patiently wait so that I do His will first and foremost in my life. Nothing else is more important.

My will and my purpose of where I go and who He wants me to become are mine to manifest with His guidance. Not everyone is meant to share their story like I am. Not everyone will be meant to help and give to others the way that I do. Nor will everyone be meant to teach others the way that I'm meant to teach. You must find your own path.

And if you think that you're on the right path that you've really found it, and it does not in any way, big or small, encompass something that helps God strengthen people and keep them on the right path and bring them to Him, then you have not found your true purpose yet.

While you have your purpose that is of the world, you also have your purpose that is of God and you must find both in order to create a balance in your life. Only attaining one will not fulfill you. We must recognize how God's purpose for each of us contributes to how we live our earthly calling.

If I was spiritually fulfilled and knew who I was in God but had no understanding of who I was supposed to be as part of the world, I probably wouldn't have the career I have nor have the knowledge that I have, which enables me to work and take care of my family. Since He knows that my spiritual understanding is not going to be enough for me to live and survive in this world of man, He makes sure that I have a proper balance between by physical body and soul so that my spiritual life can make an impact on my day-to-day life.

So, I can take care of my children, my home, and then I can go out and live my purpose because I know my home is taken care of and has no stress there. I go out into the world and do His will by bringing those who are lost back to Him by teaching those who are seeking Him what they need to know to dig deeper and find Him.

This is my path. This is my purpose. Your purpose is your own and you must seek it. And the first way to start seeking is to pick up His Book and read it. Through His Book you will gain the understanding that you need into who you are meant to be, and thus it will guide you to who you are and how you are to affect the world.

When I was younger, I always assumed that I was meant to be a lawyer. It was kind of a dream career to me. I could debate any topic and come out on top. Now that I have lived life some now and I have talent in several areas of my life, I've learned that I'm not meant to be a lawyer.

What I'm meant to be is an inspiration, a speaker, a motivator to people. I am meant to help people get to where they need to be and help them understand who they are and why they are worth so much. I am a living example to others.

Now some people would say that this fits the bill of a therapist, a psychologist, or even a social worker or a counselor. For me, those particular roles did not fit, but this does. For me to speak and hold the attention of a whole room of people is what I believe I am gifted to do. The problem that some people will encounter is that your purpose does not always stay the same.

I may be on this path for a while and God may come to me and tell me that my path has changed. I may no longer be a motivator, I may not be meant to inspire people, I may be meant to do something else, and that's okay. We must understand that the entire thought process of believing that our path is set in stone is a thought process of man. In Christ we have to understand that our path changes and we must learn to flow with the changes like water flowing down a stream. How do we know this?

If you read the Bible, you will see the disciples were all on different paths before they got on the one path with God, with Christ. They probably had no idea that this Being would come into their world and that the path that they were on would change, that they would not be doing what they were doing, but rather become disciples of the Son of God.

We even see this when people are in the midst of a calling from God. Abraham was called by God to leave his home (Genesis 12:1-2). Abraham was called to a radical life altering event. He was at a crossroads of needing to decide between abandoning everything (even family) for the sake of God.

Abraham braved this decision (granted he did not do it perfectly, bringing some people along with him), and then eventually God gives him the promise of a son, Isaac. Suddenly, God requests of Abraham to take his son to the mountain and offer him as a sacrifice. Perhaps it was here that Abraham was able to gain some empathy for the loneliness that he would have caused Hagar when he abandoned her and left her and Ishmael to fend for themselves in the desert.

Now, Abraham is ascending Mount Moriah with Isaac ready to take his son's life as commanded. Like a streak of lightening the voice of the angel comes and knocks Abraham off his path. In that split second God tells Abraham that He is pleased with his efforts and that He will bless him with the fulfilled promise of becoming a great nation.

The point we see in this is that at one moment God can be leading each of us up our own mountain and what comes with it is a feeling of definitiveness. We get so lost in the moment that we fail to see that God can work in a different way. However, we must pray, like with Abraham, that God too sends us an angel so that we can recognize when our path must change and like Isaac lying there, have faith in the change being for our greater good.

Like the disciples and Abraham, we are much the same. We must open our eyes to the fact that our path may change many times over. I could be the CEO of a company and that may be my path, then God may come to me and tell me that my path is to go into sales and my path may change again. Those who choose not to accept that the path will change and fight to stay on one path will not truly grow. They will remain stuck in that area and that's all they will ever know; there is so much more for them to learn on the other side.

So I stress to you to find your path now, but to not feel that this is the only path that you'll ever be on. Your path may change several times or may never change; however, simply be open to the fact that your path may encompass many different routes and be ready to accept this should it happen. In order to see them when He presents them to you, you must be open to the fact that they can and will come.

If you do that, you will open yourself up to a whole new world for God to work through you and whatever path He has you on. This will utterly define who you are, making you able to stand your ground and understand that change may occur and remain focused on being open to the other paths He may have for you.

Soul SCREAM: The End Was Just The Beginning
Chapter 7

I love my path. I love who I've become since I've sought Him and cried out His name. I love where He has taken me. I love the things He is showing me and the changes that He is making within me. I am full of love, understanding, and knowledge. I have been humbled to a point that I never thought that I could be humbled to simply because I sought Him, and in seeking Him He showed me the purpose of who I'm meant to be. Five years from now I, the person writing this now, will not be the same person and that's a good thing.

I open my mind to becoming more than what I am now. I used to plan my life day-by-day, week-by- week, month-by-month, and year-by-year. In the past, I could tell you exactly what my menu was going to be in my house for a whole month. Now I can't. When I started to fall back on doing this level of planning, it scared me to not know what was going to come, but what I realized was that I can't know everything. I have to have faith that God is going to show me what I need to know, as I need to know it. I'm thankful I have that level of faith now.

The things that He has shown me and the places that He has taken me so far have left me speechless. I have no doubts about the things that He will do for me and the blessings that He will give me. I have no fear of not knowing what's coming day to day. I have no fear of not knowing how I'm going to accomplish something. I literally put all of it into His hands and I just continuously tell Him that I trust Him. In doing so, He hasn't failed me yet. If He had you wouldn't be reading this book, now would you?

Find your path so that He can show you who He wants you to be, in the Spirit and in the world. Put those two together, open your mind, and be ready to take the ride of your life, because I guarantee you that once you start down His path, He will make sure that your life is more than you ever thought it could be(Romans 8:28).

Discovering who you are meant to become is not going to be easy. You'll have to hold steadfast to discovering your path. There will be many people in and around you who won't understand the path that God has set you on. Some will believe that you have or haven't changed. Some will believe that you are full of it, but stay your course no matter how hard it is or it gets.

You may lose friends, family, and people whom you thought cared about you and whom you cared about as well. However, don't worry or get upset because God will send the people that you need to help you on your path. They will strengthen you, help you, and assist you you in keeping your focus.

Those are the people that will be in your life for the days, maybe even years to come. There are other people who are doing the same thing you're doing and they'll stay around you to lift you up when you fall as you'll do the same for them.

If you become dismayed, cry and learn to let it go. Just because some can't understand who you are or whom you're becoming doesn't mean that God is done working with them. He may still have things in progress in them and their lives. They may come your path again and you might have to be a catalyst for helping them change, but they may also never cross your path again and that's okay too.

We have to understand that the people we want in our lives may not be the people He, our Father above, wants in our lives. That can be a hard pill to swallow sometimes. I've been on this path moving towards becoming who I am meant to be and, yet, my ex-husband and I are still unable to be friends nor is he willing to co-parent with me. While this is unfortunate, I still have to stay on my path.

I lost a very close friend from my childhood, yet I have to stay on my path. I lost a friend who was more like a sister who was very close to me that doesn't believe that this is who I really am, but I have to stay on my path.

If I change my path to accommodate the things and people of the world, then I am no long on God's path for me, but the path of the people and the world around me. This you cannot let happen, you have got to stay steadfast on YOUR path. Accept your losses, because God will send many gains (Mark 10:29-30).

Accept who you are because you're beautiful. Don't look for where you're going because He will show you that in time. This is what makes following Jesus as the Way, the Truth, and the Life such a pivotal moment in everyone's lives (John 14:6).

CHAPTER {8}

LESSON 5: SURROUND YOURSELF WITH THE RIGHT PEOPLE OF ACCOUNTABILITY

Listen to advice and accept instruction, that you may gain wisdom for the future. (Proverbs 19:20)

#

Had I known this lesson sooner, that I needed to surround myself with the right people of accountability, I can't even imagine how much more developed I could've been before I got and while I was married. I had so many friends and I could count hundreds of people who knew me. Some I classified as friends and some I classified as associates.

Now, I had a particular friend who was a friend since childhood. He was a great friend while I was a child, through high school, and even into my early twenties. All my life I gave one hundred percent of myself to him and our friendship. I looked past things that I wouldn't normally look past, I forgave things that I normally wouldn't have forgiven for anyone else. I did things for him that I normally wouldn't do for anyone else.

When I got divorced this person was right there with me and he had my back one hundred percent of the way. The only problem was that I felt that there were times that he was not as good of a friend to me as I was to him. I'll come back to this in a moment.

A problem like this comes when we start to change or mature, or our friends start to change or mature, and we are no longer on the same playing field in our lives, in our emotional and/or spiritual development. When I was in my twenties and dating my soon-to-be husband I was very promiscuous, with him of course. But looking back now, I realize that my reasoning for doing this wasn't because I was in love with him, but because I wanted him to be in love with me and there is a difference.

A lot of the behaviors I exhibited back then, my friends had no problem with. The people around me didn't say anything, except my parents. My mother wasn't very pleased with the decisions I was making in life, she was one who would never hold her tongue and always made it very clear how she felt. Like some people, I could have just cut my mom off and stopped dealing with her and stopped listening to her, but what I realized was that my mother really loved me.

In my twenties I came to the conclusion that even though I was not necessarily living life the way I should be or the way she would want me to be living it, I was fully aware of it and I was accepting of it. I was willing to compromise on morals and values that my parents had spent thousands of dollars sending me to private school to instill in me. Those morals and values went out the window when I went out of the house and out into the world.

I just realized that if I wanted to get what I wanted, then I was going to have to make compromises. So, I changed my personality, I changed my activities, I changed the whole way I thought and the way I lived my life in order to please the people that were around me in order to fit in.

By the time I got divorced, I had pretty much disassociated myself from my own family (my intermediate siblings and parents). I still worked with my mom during the week part-time off and on, but I really didn't communicate with my family or spend time with my family like I used to. I had become so wrapped up in my ex- husband's family and, because I saw my family as not being what I thought it should be, I decided to pull away from my family and make his family my own.

That honestly was the worst decision; I will say that there were some members that were more critical of me than others, but I do not harbor any ill will towards them or any resentment because I truly do believe that some of the things they did and said, were done as a means to promote positive growth and behavior in me. At least, that's what I believe in my heart that they were trying to do.

It's unfortunate that I didn't realize any of that back then. Their actions produced a negative response in me and as a parent I learned first hand how. The way you deal with your child or other people may work for some, but as you get older it may not work for others. This is why people come in and out of your life, because you change, they change and the ways in which you relate or communicate with them may not adapt so easily.

When I got divorced, because of the affair I was shunned initially. In the beginning, my husband's family did try to include me and keep me in the picture as to not choose sides and isolate the children. Unfortunately, they had no choice but to change that. He was so hurt that having me around was not a good thing at all for him, his behavior nor mine at times. It caused him to be more argumentative and that caused me to always be on the defensive and argue back. In the end they decided that they had to make a choice.

Now, the only problem I had with this was that I felt that when they made their choice, they held me accountable for certain actions and behaviors that they didn't hold him accountable for. I felt like he was the victim, the martyr in all of this, and they enabled this by not bringing to his attention his actions and behaviors which provoked or made situations worse.

Whether they did that because they felt like he wasn't responsible for anything or that nothing he had done in our marriage had contributed to my decisions and actions as to why I ended up cheating, I don't know. What I do know is that they chose to condemn me and in condemning me I felt like he actually got closer to his family, based on this foundation of negativity centered around me and everyone's opinion of my actions.

Even a year or more later I'd see one of his family members somewhere and they wouldn't speak to me, yet these were the people who were my family for fifteen years. So how are you a family member for fifteen years, and immediately after a divorce you are no longer a part of the family? I don't quite understand that because my family isn't like that.

When my cousin got divorced he had children and he got custody of his children fifty percent of the time. We would see his ex-wife and we would still speak to her. We simply never judge anybody or harbor any ill will toward anybody because we don't know the whole story involved in a particular situation, we never will and honestly, it's none of our business. It was their marriage not ours.

However, the fact of the matter is, since it was he who brought her into this family in the first place, there was something that he absolutely must have loved about her, and the fact that she is now the mother of his children means that there was even more that he absolutely adored about the woman to have children with her.

And one thing about my family is we never neglect, abandon or mistreat any children in our family no matter what the reason the parents are no longer together. The kids are still always included in all family functions.

We never felt the need to destroy my cousin's ex mentally or emotionally. We might gossip about the things that transpired causing the end to their marriage, but we definitely would not put that person down or judge them based on what little we knew about the entire situation.

When I didn't receive this same unbiased love from his family, I literally felt lost, confused and devastated. The decision that I had made to pull away from my family and become closer to my husband's literally became the worst decision I had ever made. I never should have walked away from my family. I never should have doubted in any way shape or form my family's ability to love me through any and everything I was going to go through.

After all of this was said and done, I was in some ways put out of his family. I had to walk away from his family and go back to mine. Now, if you notice, I didn't say go crawling back because I didn't have to go back crawling to my family, they literally welcomed me with open arms

I won't say that they didn't scold me, they did a little, but at the same time they were so open to having me back and being able to love me and heal me that, while it was a hard thing for me to swallow my pride and admit that I was wrong, I ended up going back willingly and lovingly.

The years that I was married, some of the people that I surrounded myself with were fantastic, and some of them weren't. Once I got divorced and I started reading the Word and understanding more of who I was supposed to be, I started taking more accountability for my actions and how my actions played into my divorce.

The more I did that, the more I realized that the people I was surrounding myself with were not the people that I wanted to surround myself with to have the right influence on me to help foster the woman I now knew I wanted to become.

You know that old adage: "When you see somebody's friends, it will tell you what kind of person they really are." Basically, that saying came into play, and as I started to become closer to God and read the Word and understand who I was supposed to be, I took a look around at the people I was surrounding myself with and I realized that they were people that couldn't foster in me what God was trying to do with me. These people were hindering what God was trying to do.

What they failed to realize was that when you don't hold someone accountable for certain behaviors if they're at fault, whether by words or actions, they can't grow. They'll continue to do that same act over and over again because no one has brought it to their attention that their acting in an unhealthy and wrong way.

It's like a dog that goes into the trash; the dog will keep going in the trash continuously because no one is telling the dog that it is wrong. A good pet owner knows that you are supposed to make sure that the dog doesn't get into the trash and you are supposed to teach him that it's wrong. This is where your friends and the people you surround yourself come into play.

Soul SCREAM: The End Was Just The Beginning
Chapter 8

You want to surround yourself with people who are going to hold you accountable for the level of person you want to be. You do not want to be around people who are going to enable your bad behaviors. At thirty-five years old I got divorced and found out that a lot of the behaviors that I had been exhibiting my whole thirty-five years (and during my fifteen year relationship) was really bad and immature behavior. Nobody had ever dared tell me this before because they feared my attitude, my venomous words and tantrums.

There were a lot of things I saw while growing up, so I took these behaviors from other people I observed during my life. I had never seen anybody correct them on it, so I adopted their habits and took them with me into my adult life. Then in my adult life no one corrected me either.

Part of it is that if you correct one person on a bad habit, then you really have to look at yourself to see if you are doing it yourself as well and correct yourself as well.

I can honestly say that these people who were surrounding me were doing a lot of the same things that I was doing. It was more of a "Do as I say, not as I do" kind of thing. Still, I don't hold it against any of them. What I had a hard time learning was that when I started to grow, I was actually capable of catching the bad behaviors in myself and keeping myself from doing certain things and stopping before I stepped off the curb into behaviors that I now knew were not acceptable.

I find the number one reason why people do not make others accountable for bad behaviors is that they do not want to lose that person as a friend, a family member, or someone that they care about. The problem with this is that a person's fear of not wanting to lose someone's friendship or communication in the physical means that a lack of challenging the other person prevents them from receiving the challenges that will assist them to develop mentally, emotionally and spiritually in the physical.

Now, as I started to see certain behaviors within myself and was able to catch them I started maturing, growing and progressing. As I changed, people were used to me being a certain way for so long that they weren't able to neither believe nor accept the new person that I was showing myself to be. They thought it was a phase or a temporary lapse of personality. In actuality, I was really progressing but they had never seen me in this capacity before.

What happened over time was that I chose to walk away from some of those friends and family members. The friend that I mentioned in the opening paragraph sadly fell into this category. I decided that I could not be surrounded by people who were not going to foster in me the things that I needed in order to grow. If there was a behavior that I was exhibiting, I needed the people around me to tell me, because I wasn't as knowledgeable in some areas I needed to develop in as others were.

Soul SCREAM: The End Was Just The Beginning
Chapter 8

Since I lost so many friends and family members in the divorce, my friends that remained were limited. One friend had been there from the time before my marriage up until today. She has been a constant rock and a constant force in my progression and I love her for this.

I was also blessed enough to come across another friend after my divorce when I moved back to Delaware. She also gained my respect as one of the two people in my life who could tell me when I was wrong and whose judgment I could trust.

See, on top of holding people accountable for their actions and helping them in the right areas, you yourself need to be strong in that area in order to do so. If I have no patience, then I can't teach somebody else patience. This was what I was experiencing with my friends. There were some areas of my life that I was highly developed in, but the areas I wasn't yet developed in that these some of my closest friends came into the picture and started to develop me in, as well as others.

Their way was not to criticize me for my behaviors, choices, or decisions, instead they used different methods of showing me what choice I made, action I took, how I ended up with unfavorable results (or results I didn't want), and how I could go back and improve my decision making process. They literally became my teachers in several facets of my life and through them I started to meet more people that I absolutely adored and loved having around me.

Chapter 8

My friend "Santha" is the one I credit with introducing me to my Apostle Raymond Stansbury of Prophetic House of Truth Outreach, who lead me to discovering another piece of the puzzle to the part I play in God's purpose for man. In this ministry she and I have grown tremendously in leaps and bounds. If it wasn't for Santha, there were many days I would have given up on progressing and seeking spiritual guidance because I became so discouraged at times.

She is my no nonsense friend. She's got your back but if you bring too much foolishness her way, she won't waste her time telling you over and over what's wrong concerning you and your actions. Then she'll eventually leave you to your own devices but keep the Band-Aids and tissue ready when you come needing your wounds cleaned and your tears wiped and she'll patch up lovingly.

My friend "Mara" has just recently entered back into my life. We went to high school together and then lost touch. But recently God made our paths cross again and she has been an encouraging and stabilizing force in my life. When my over analytical brain starts turning and making some situation more than it is, Maya has a way of pulling me back to my focus, ME. She has been pivotal in the last few weeks of getting this book, my baby, out to the world.

Soul SCREAM: The End Was Just The Beginning
Chapter 8

See what I mean? Maybe we both had some growing to do the years we were apart but when the time was right God brought her and I back into each other's lives and the lessons I'm getting from her are new and just as valuable as the ones I got from my other friends these past years.

My friend "Kell" was able to show me where I was immature in some of the ways that I thought, my emotions, and even sometimes my mental status. She didn't criticize me for it, she was simply there to help me acknowledge the areas where I needed work and to give me guidance on how to work on those areas. Unfortunately, she and I are no longer in touch but that does not diminish in any way, shape or form what she has taught me and the how much I valued our friendship.

My one friend "Nesha" fostered me and helped me grow in the area of dealing with and speaking to people with less arrogance, understanding how people were perceiving my words and actions. When I make decisions or when I take actions, Nesha makes me accountable and aware of things that I do and how people were affected by them.

The thing that makes Nesha so special is that even when she is getting frustrated or struggling to have patience with me, which can be a challenge at times, she still does so and is pretty animated and funny while doing it. She makes me laugh at myself and sometimes in life you need that.

My friend "Kia" I absolutely love too. Kia is actually Nesha's cousin and Kia fostered me in the area of single parenting. She taught me how to take the things that my kids had and wanted and use them as a tool in disciplining them and encouraging them to behave properly and to work for what they wanted.

And the nice thing about Kia is she is straightforward and real. If she said it, she meant it and she taught me to parent with this same approach so I could get results when disciplining my kids, instilling strong morals and values, and following through.

My friend "Angela" my big sister and isn't afraid to check me when I'm out of hand. She is my source of accountability on my behavior and actions in situations dealing with relationships and family. I used to become very defensive with men and strike like a cobra with venomous mean words.

Angela helped me see that not all men are like my ex or some of the other men I dated and identified traits that I could look for that would allow me to feel safe, let my guard down some or kick the guy to the curb, when necessary. Trust me, she knows her stuff, is a great judge of character and many have been left sitting on the curb with no regrets, thanks to her guidance. She has been my mentor and saving grace when it comes to surviving the dating world again.

And last but not least, the friend that has been with me through any and everything, "Latoya". This friend has literally been around since I was an infant because our mothers have been

Soul SCREAM: The End Was Just The Beginning
Chapter 8

friends since before we were born. She is more of a sister than a friend. Our kids have grown up together and there's a funny story behind that. Every time she or I got pregnant the other ended up pregnant. We didn't plan it that way but to this day our mothers still believe we may have.

This woman and her husband were there before my ex and I ever met. She and I can go months or years without talking and just pick up the phone and act like it's only been hours. She's the friend I fought as a kid and then turned around and we iced each other's bruises. She is one of the most important because she's my rock. No matter what, I know I can always call on her to confide in or give me words of encouragement when needed.

She's known me from the beginning and has watched me grow and evolve in every way and I will always love her dearly no matter what we go through.

These seven women over the years have been absolutely pivotal in my life. While I have a lot of people who have played a major part, these people played and play the biggest part right now.

One last person I have to give credit to is going to shock you, but I must keep it real and truthful. I have to give credit to Cameron and here's why. Cam saw beauty in me when I couldn't see any at all in myself. I was at a point in life where I was questioning my worth and purpose. I had attached those things along with my beauty to my husband and how he looked at and treated me. So when he stopped looking at me, being intimate and emotionally detached from me I felt like I had no worth anymore.

Cameron used to tell me all the time how he valued our friendship over the years, how he appreciated me, how I valued him and who I was as a person. I not only used the negative words my husband spoke to see my true worth and value, I used Cameron's words as well. I think had I gone through a divorce without the affair happening, and me being able to see my value through Cameron's eyes, I definitely would have had a harder time surviving it.

The fact that he saw worth and beauty in me at the lowest point in my self-esteem still amazes me. If he saw me today I think he would be very proud of the woman I've become. He lit a spark in me and I put the gasoline to his spark and have made it blaze like never before within myself. And I have to admit, I'm also very proud of me.

So, when it comes to growing and learning and maturing in different areas in your life, you need to pick different types of people of accountability. The most important thing you want to do is pick the right people of accountability. You don't want people who are going to criticize you for your poor mistakes, or your poor judgments; you need people who are going to absolutely, positively relay to you the areas that you need to work on and the things that you need to improve upon.

Finding these people is going to be a process and it is not going to be easy. It may take you longer than I did (or maybe sooner). I was lucky because some of them were in my life already and from that one I got additional ones. One of them I just happened upon when I moved into my neighborhood and she became a really great friend. I have many people of accountability in my life; I could sit here and list the names endlessly. These seven were the pivotal ones along with everybody else that worked with them.

I no longer take complete credit for who I am; I am who I am because God has allowed these people to come into my life and to show me the things that I was previously too blind to see. I truly believe that it is because God has helped them grow in these areas that they have been able to help me grow in each of the areas as well.

People will come and go in and out of your life. The one thing that you do want to pay attention to is who they are, what they bring with them, and when they leave, what they might have left you with. This is because what they come with definitely should be an asset to who you are and where you are in life. When they leave, they should leave you with the knowledge and the lessons that you need to know in order to continue to move ahead.

If someone comes into your life and you cannot figure out what they are bringing into it, let me stress this to you: You may not be able to see what they are bringing initially, but over time it will be made clear to you if you pray on it and you ask God to show you. If you get the answer that they are not bringing anything to your life that fulfills you and helps you grow, then you need to acknowledge that it may not be best for you to stay in that particular friendship or relationship; it just may not be the best thing for you.

I have many people who have come into my life for a season and for a reason, and with every single one of them I have been able to recognize what they brought in and what they left when they left.

I now have a selection process that allows me to be around people for a shorter period of time in order to come to the determination of what they are bringing and leaving. I believe that this is a gift from God. I believe that this is blessing that He has literally strengthened in me in order to create a revolving door for those who do not need to be in my life, those who do not foster positivity, maturity and growth. I am thankful for that revolving door.

I will say that I have met some amazing people, but there are always some people who still need some work. The one thing that I will say is that I don't have any enemies (in my opinion) that I have ever made. I try to leave every relationship or encounter that I have with someone on a positive note. Just because I choose not to have someone in my life as a person of accountability does not mean that I don't like them or that they're not a nice person.

It may mean that they can't be in my life because God may want them to be in someone else's life. He may want them to be a person of accountability for someone else and not for me. Consequently, I don't get upset when people walk out of my life, nor do I get upset when I have to turn and walk away. I believe that God is teaching us that regardless of who comes in and out of my life, at the end of the day, as long as you hold steadfast to Him and His love, we will be whole and fulfilled.

CHAPTER {9}

YOU'LL FEEL BETTER AFTER YOU SCREAM

#

The last chapter of any book I feel is one of the most important.

For me, the last chapter sums up everything that the book is about and puts it in a neat little package with a bow on top. It took me over a month to write this last chapter. The words and the thoughts and emotions were all inside me, I just couldn't figure out how to share them with everyone. Many times I thought that I was finished writing this book, and then another chapter suddenly appeared out of nowhere from within my mind.

Now, in light of recent events that have taken place, and in the midst of this book being written, I finally have found what needs to be said in this last chapter.

Words that are spoken are very strong, they can be positive words or they can be negative words, or sometimes they could just be words that truly are said with no intended purpose or end result. During the course of my metamorphosis, determining who I want to be and learning how to get there, I had a lot of things that were said to me, and even now I have had things said to me that just rattle around in my head and have become somewhat of an essence to who I am.

The words unfortunately hurt very much when originally spoken, but now I am thankful that they were. I truly do give credit to these words, helping me find my path and helping to keep me on it.

"You will never change, you're not capable of change, you will always be the same person you've always been, and no good will come to you."

These were the words that were spoken to me on the day my husband left. And after those words were said, I sat down and I cried, but not because of these words, but because of what I was losing in that one moment when the words were spoken and because I actually believed about myself what was said.

It wasn't until a year later, after playing these words back in my head over and over again trying to find a hidden message of hope in there somewhere that my marriage could be saved, that I realized the true meaning of these words. I don't know whether or not the words were spoken in an attempt to hurt me, or from his own pain, but a year later I took these words and I wrote them on my wall in my bedroom and I looked at them every day.

Like I shared before, I made these words one of the first things I saw in the morning, and I would read them to myself. It was one of the last things I would see at night, and I would read them to myself.

I have decided I will never say these words or words like it to anybody, not even people who hurt me.

I held onto these words because I said to myself, "I never want to hear somebody say these words to me again, so I am going to read these words, say these words, repeat these words to myself, and I am going to work on who I am and who I want to be and try to be a better person, so that when I hear these words, if I should ever have to hear these words in the future, I shall now know that these words are not true and no longer apply to me."

To think that someone is incapable of change is sad and disappointing. Our whole Christian faith is built upon the belief that, with Christ's guidance, we are capable of becoming all that we are meant to be in God's eyes and that we are able to be whatever we believe we can become. I believe that God focused on this so much in the Bible because He knew how hard it would be for us to remember this and practice this with the free will and emotions that we would be experiencing.

I look around me from the bum on the street to the addict on the corner to the alcoholic with the beer bottle, and I no longer look at these people as a lost cause; every soul is savable, and every person is capable of change. Helping them find that path is what I believe my purpose is in life. I am on my own path, true. And, yes, I do step off and get back on many times, but that's the key, I get back on. Some people step off and they don't know how to get back on how, they don't know how to change, they don't know how to start, restart or they've fallen so much that they've just given up and they feel like there's nothing else they can do.

They feel like that they've fallen so far that they can't come back from something, but the truth is, in someone else's eyes, you may not be able to, but in God's eyes and mine you can do anything. With God, and the guidance that Christ offers, we can come back from anything in our life and become a better person than we were before. And that is what I did. I used my hurt, my pain, and these words which were spoken to me by him to do just that. I worked on me. It was the only thing that I could do, so I did it.

Learning to focus on me and make me a priority wasn't a very easy lesson to learn after living to please others for so long in my life. It was very difficult. Even now I still struggle with wanting to prove to others, including my ex, that I've changed, but I no longer feel the need to try. I can't worry about what other people say if they're not willing to see me for who I now am. Those who want to live in the past can, however I no longer do and no longer want to. Life is short and I still have a lot to accomplish still. I can't allow myself to be hindered by these people who don't want to see me or know me for who I really am.

It is unfortunate, but my ex-husband and I have no communication. One reason is because I believe that we are incapable of communicating with each other at this point because of all the things that transpired in the past.

I've changed and I've grown in a lot of ways, and I've tried to reach out to him in order to co-parent with him in order to provide a better environment for our children; unfortunately, he has stressed to me that he does not want to co-parent with me. So, regardless of what I believe to be the best for our children, I can't give them that on my own so.

So I focus on doing what I can do by myself, being the best role model and the best example that I can be to them and enjoying the awesome relationship I have built with them over the years. I came from a two parent home, so I didn't know the first thing about being a single parent but I surrounded myself with the right people and influences so I could become a stronger and more rounded parent to meet as many of their parental needs as I could.

I don't know what their relationship is with their father on his side when they're with him, but I take faith in knowing that when they come home I will be sharing with them the lessons that I've learned in my life from day to day.

I think the biggest injustice as a parent, is when we as adults learn something, whether it is from making a mistake, or just growing in general, and we don't share with our children what we learn. I'm a different type of parent. Anybody who knows me who's around my children will tell you that I parent a lot differently than most people. I believe that parenting should be customized to each child.

So, while my roles are the same, my discipline is different for each child. But the biggest thing that I do pride myself on is that when I learn something, or I learn from something I've done wrong, I let my kids know. And when they tell me, "Mom, you were wrong," and if I was truly wrong, I have no problem admitting to them that, yes, I was.

I do this because I don't want them to go through life feeling they must be "perfect", not being able to admit when they are wrong and putting more emphasis on the fact that they're angry that someone brought it to their fault to their attention.

Instead of putting energy in that, they need to be focused on acknowledging that they were wrong and what they're going to do to create: to learn from it and to become better. That is what I want them to be focused on, and that is what they are now currently focused on.

How people see you and perceive you is not always going to be determined by you. I have changed so much, and I have been lucky to have a lot of great people around me who have acknowledged it. But, unfortunately, I am never in the presence of my ex-husband for him to experience who I am now.

It would have helped for both of us to have been able to be open to getting to know each other again, just to be able to give our kids an environment where both of their parents are sitting at their graduation or their wedding and they don't have to feel stressed about it.

Regardless, in the end, they have learned and they've seen a lot of things and understand a lot more than most children their age, and while I may never have a civil relationship or friendship of any sort with their father, I hold nothing but blessings and prayers for him. He put a lot of faith into me, and hopefully he finds someone one day who will not disappoint him like I did. I know now that I was only human, so mistakes will be made. I need to be with a person who understands that and is willing to accept that there is no such thing as perfection.

I thank God every day that I have made the changes that my ex-husband said I wasn't capable of, and I am happy with everything that God has blessed me with. I believe that I had to lose everything in order to gain more than I had before, and I didn't just gain it in knowledge and maturity, I gained it in grace and favor. And, honestly, those two things can truly have no price put on how much they are worth in your life.

While I'm not perfect in this area yet and never will be, I try to no longer live based on my emotions or act based on my emotions. While I have my emotions, I choose to live above and beyond what I feel. I don't have to feel patient to be patient. I don't have to feel forgiveness to be forgiving. Forgiveness is not about letting something go; it is how you choose to treat the person after the event has happened.

Soul SCREAM: The End Was Just The Beginning
Chapter 9

There is a second quote that used to run through my head and try to defeat me:

"I don't like you. I don't want to like you. I don't want to feel anything about you."

These words also hurt very deeply. Before I was his wife, I was his friend, and honestly through this whole endeavor, losing my friend was what hurt more than anything else. But what I realized with these words was that regardless of how much I've changed, there were things that I did do. Whether they were because I was immature, or because I was selfish, or because I had walked away from my faith, the reason doesn't matter.

The fact is the actions and words in the past before I changed were not nice. And while I've had several people come in and out of my life, some who have stayed around long enough to witness my growth through Christ, there are those who haven't stuck around. I may have to cross paths again with these people someday, and I realize now that I will forever have to deal with the consequences of my actions and my words from my past self.

How do you do that? How do you survive when you've worked so hard to change who you are and every now and then you go around a corner and there is someone there who has condemned you for who you used to be and the things that you've done?

How do you stay on your path, how do you not get angry, how do you not resent this person for being able to see who you are now? And how do you not give up on continuing to grow and learn when it looks like nobody can see your growth but you and God?

I'll tell you how you do it. You apologize for the things that you've done, and then you turn around and walk away. And you keep walking to where you are going. You can't control what people think about you or say about you at all. It is what they are going to do. But you can be the bigger person and not let somebody's actions or emotions knock you off your spiritual foundation. This is why my relationship with God was the most quintessential thing in helping me to change and embark upon a new path.

This is why I truly believe that God did not send my ex-husband back. In the beginning I was very, very upset that He did not change his heart and send him back to me, but now I am glad, because I understand that had He sent him back to me, I never would have evolved into the woman I am today and I'm pretty amazing.

I would have gotten so wrapped up in my ex-husband being back, the physical pleasure of him being home would have wrapped me up so much, that I would have stopped praying, stopped going to church, and stop trying to learn and grow.

Something I've learned through this is that physical happiness and pleasure is temporary. It in no way touches true joy and happiness, which is given to us through our relationship with Christ. I tell people all the time, "Please don't try to steal my joy, because you can't, it will be a futile attempt, but if you reach out to me I will share my joy with you and I will even show you how I got it."

I will have other relationships, I may get married again, but my relationship with God will be my first and foremost relationship in my life. Regardless of who comes and goes into my life from now on, I know that God will be there.

He will never come second to my children, he will never come second to my husband, and he will never come second to me. He will be my first priority always, and anything else and anyone else in my life will only be an accent to make that relationship with Him so much better.

The diagram on the next page I actually came up with to basically show how I now view my relationship with God and the people around me. Take a close look and you'll see that in the center of the main circle with my name is a smaller circle. That very center circle is God.

He is the core of everything and everyone. He is the core of me, and I exist because of Him.

The smaller dots that are on the outside of me, these are the people who accentuate my life, like my friends I told you about. That's why each circle has an initial in it for them. Take notice that if you take one of those dots from the outside of the border that represents me, I am still whole, I am still intact.

In order to remove that small center circle, God, from the center of me would mean breaking the border that is me. In other words, taking God from me would destroy and weaken me and I would no longer be whole nor leave a strong solid border of support for my friends and family around me. I would be empty; there would be nothing there at the center to build around and my border could be taped up or mended but would never be as strong as before.

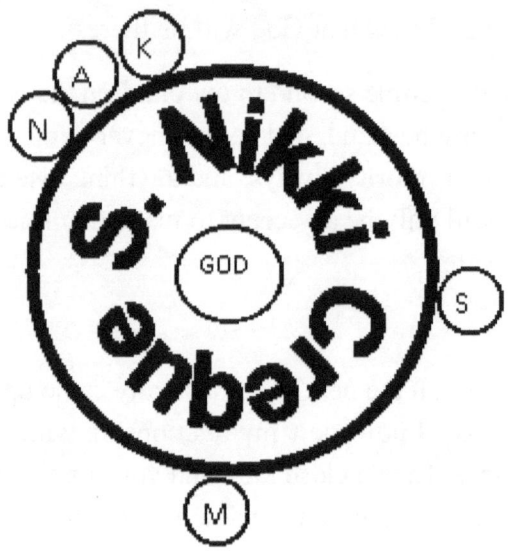

We must understand that God is the core of who we are and everybody else in our lives, they're just an accent that He gives to us. The people He brings into our lives, they are sent to us to make our lives more enjoyable, to make our lives happy in the physical. But all of these emotions and things that we feel, He could choose to have us feel these things without people if He wants.

So we must be thankful for all that He gives us and all the people that He puts around us, because the people that He chooses to be around us are gifts from Him. I am thankful every day for my amazing friends and the people who are around me.

Every single one of them has taught me something that has allowed me to grow and become a better person, a stronger person, a wiser person, a more beautiful person. And I am thankful every day for Him allowing me to have these people in my life.

And should He decide that any of these people have to go for any reason, that they will not be my friend anymore, then I will be thankful for all that I've learned from them and all that I've gotten from them, and I will continue on my path with Him to where He needs me to go, regardless of who is by my side or who is with me. This is all He asks of us. This is all He asks.

So as I draw a close to this chapter of my life, I invite all of you to seek out the things that you need to change. You may not be able to see them, you may not be able to feel them; you will only be able to find out through Him.

I implore you to ask Him to show you, but what He shows you I ask you to be open to receiving what He says and what He shows you and understand that your emotions may try to stop that growth, but you have to think outside of them in order to continue to grow, and I implore you to do this.

Soul SCREAM: The End Was Just The Beginning
Chapter 9

I am not perfect at this, I am still learning, there are so many lessons that I am going through, and so many emotions that I am learning to control and live with, but the fact is I know that I have to learn this, so I continue to do what I need to do in order to learn it. In particular, I have had to learn to adjust to life without a husband. I don't dislike nor do I hate my ex-husband.

He's not the person that I used to know, but he is still an amazing individual. And the woman that he ends up with, well, hopefully she will be the one that God sends to him. I have my opinion of some of the things He said and some of the things He's done, but my opinion is irrelevant. The only opinion that truly matters is God's.

I no longer feel the need to gain approval of those who don't approve of me or my actions in the past. I no longer try to prove to anyone who I am in Christ's name. I feel that if He wants someone to know He'll show them, and I might be around when He shows them, but I might not be.

I may never know that He has shown them, or I might never cross that person's path if He sees fit to make that happen. But at the end of the day, I try to live more as God's child, than as a mere human being. Before I am Nikki, I am His child.

I have received that and acknowledged that, and I'm proud to be so. I know that in writing this book I share my weaknesses as a person, but I also share my growth. There will be some who will condemn me for what I did: the affair, the lying, and the manipulation.

Soul SCREAM: The End Was Just The Beginning
Chapter 9

I can honestly say that it's because of my relationship with God and the teachings of Christ that I'm prepared to stand on my spiritual foundation and take every blow that will come my way, every negative comment and every rude remark I am ready to take.

I am shielded by His grace, and I will not be knocked off my foundation. My emotions will no longer control my actions. And while there are those people who will doubt whether or not God is real or whether or not Christ truly existed, I don't feel I need to fight to argue the truth of these two things, for it will be how I live and how I treat others that people will get to see a testimony to God's work.

What will be, will be. We have to live our lives to see what that is.

I pray that every soul who picks up this book and reads it finds something in it that awakens another part of who they are. And after everything is said and done, after you've been through everything you can go through, and you are now seeking something and you are not sure what it is, I hope that you will reach out to Him, because I can tell you that He will show you what it is that you seek.

He will show you how He's your missing piece. And just like me, I know that you'll feel better after you let your Soul Scream.

FROM THE AUTHOR

After losing so much and becoming so lost, I went in the book store seeking a book about affairs, divorce and how to start healing. All the books I found were written by the person whom had been cheated on. I was unsuccessful in finding a book about how to facilitate healing and growth for a remorseful cheater.

When I embarked upon this journey of self-healing and growth, I had no idea that God would instruct me to share my story. It took a lot of courage for me to do just that and some days I question if people even believe a cheater can truthfully be remorseful.

What you have just read and encountered is a part of my soul, which Thomas and I have worked long and hard to put into words in order for you to truly feel my pain, hurt, joy, happiness and share my transformation with the world.

Each day is a day that I continue to awake and ask God to touch me with His knowledge, guidance, patience, and endurance. I have no intention of changing this, though life sometimes presents challenges that knock me off course from time to time, which I am sure is the same for you.

And while others may judge you for the slips or falls you will have and endure, I need you to remember one thing:

Soul SCREAM: The End Was Just The Beginning
From The Author

You're not perfect. So get up, brush yourself off, keep moving, learning and growing.

There is no such thing as a perfect or conflict free life or a perfect relationship. While you should want to avoid being the source of these things, you must remember that it is in the storm that we have the greatest opportunity to grow and learn if we remain open to it.

I urge you to read God's word in the Bible, seek professional help, and find a group of encouraging people who are going to help you grow and not just critique your growth. The Bible I recommend is The Complete Jewish Bible by David H. Stern. It is the most complete translation with less removed passages removed, that I've found so far.

Everybody's learning style is different. Unlike some, I am able to learn better when my lesson is being conveyed to me in a peaceful and calm manner, which allows me to feel as though I am being heard as well. Take the time to pray and ask God to help you determine yours.

And I know many people have one question they want to ask and that is: After four years, how are things with your ex-husband now?

Let me start by saying that the person I was married to was an amazing person, man, provider, father, and friend. The one regret that I do have is that I didn't know or appreciate all of these attributes until I no longer had him in my life. Who he is now I don't know, but what I do know is that God's plan is always greater than our own.

And if it is meant for us to know each other again as parents of these three amazingly beautiful kids we have, then we will. But if He doesn't feel it is necessary for me to accomplish the things He has set out for me, then I'm good with that as well.

Learning to accept that God's plan may not always coincide with mine was not easy, but it has brought a sense of peace to my life that I hadn't known before. My life is an automobile owned by Him, and sometimes it has a mind of its own and takes twists and turns that I didn't plot out on my map.

The nice thing is that I trust Him explicitly and have complete faith in every route He has me headed on. When you reach this level of faith, you will start to see that some things and people of the world can do nothing to weaken it, and you will always find a way to smile through the hurt, the pain, and even the anger.

Soul SCREAM: The End Was Just The Beginning
From The Author

When I was married I created a cute game that I use to play to try and keep my husband guessing. The name of the game was:

W.I.D.B.I.L.Y.

What

I

Do Because

I

Love

You

I would write this word on pieces of paper and hide them around the house, in the car or any secret spontaneous hiding place for him to find. It wasn't until after our marriage ended that I realized that I had put more energy into showing him I loved him than I did into showing myself I loved me.

Never again will I make this mistake. I'm actually in the process of creating bracelets that I will be releasing to the public for any and everybody to wear to remind themselves to put time into loving you first.

It's my wish that every little girl, woman and even men learn this word and apply it to themselves and spend a little more time spoiling and catering to themselves from time to time. I'm not stranger to people telling me I'm conceded.

My reply to that statement is, "I am and you should be too." I believe everyone is entitled to a little conceit as long as they're not putting others down in the process. I love me, I'm in love with loving me and you should be too.

Thank you for allowing me to share my amazing journey with you. It doesn't end here. I have so much more to awaken you to as He awoke in me. And, remember, no matter what you've done and where you are, I still believe in you and your ability to keep growing spiritually, emotionally, and mentally.

Next time you slip or fall and you're brushing yourself off, take a look to your right, you may see me right next to you on one knee brushing myself off as well, about to take off running again as quickly as I can.

Never forget, forgive yourself first and foremost and then leave the rest up to God.

Shaniika "Nikki" Creque

www.nikkicreque.com

www.ingramcontent.com/pod-product-compliance
Lightning Source LLC
Chambersburg PA
CBHW031423290426
44110CB00011B/494